Socks

CHRISSIE DAY

GUILD OF MASTER
CRAFTSMAN PUBLICATIONS

First published 2008 by
Guild of Master Craftsman Publications Ltd
Castle Place, 166 High Street,
Lewes, East Sussex BN7 1XU

Text and Designs © Chrissie Day, 2008
© In the Work, GMC Publications Ltd, 2008.

ISBN: 978-1-86108-616-7

A catalogue record of this book is available from
the British Library.

Charts and pattern checking by Carol Chambers
Knitting and crochet illustrations by Simon Rodway

Associate Publisher: Jonathan Bailey
Managing Editor: Gerrie Purcell
Production Manager: Jim Bulley
Editor: Alison Howard
Managing Art Editor: Gilda Pacitti
Design & Photography: Rebecca Mothersole

Set in Gill Sans and Ribbon

Colour origination by **GMC Reprographics**
Printed and bound by Kyodo Printing in Singapore

Why we love socks

Everyone needs something to keep their feet warm,
so socks are an ideal project for any knitter.
A hand-knitted sock is a pleasure to own and will always
outlive its commercially produced poor relation.
Small and worked in one piece, socks are a perfectly portable
work in progress that can be done at any time of the year.
While everyone is scampering about barefoot in the warmth
of summer, why not knit some socks in cheerful colours to
keep out the winter chills?

All the socks in this book are worked entirely or partly using
double-pointed or circular needles, in a variety of yarns. If you
are keen to try knitting in the round, you are ready to start
making socks. In the pages ahead, you will find patterns for all
ages and all occasions, including methods for different styles
of heel and toe.

Enjoy.

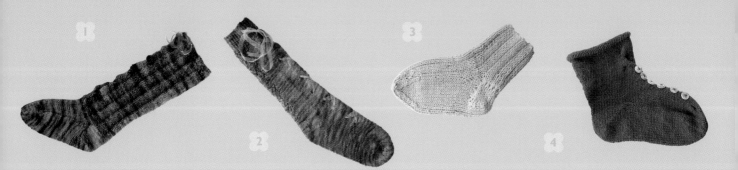

Contents

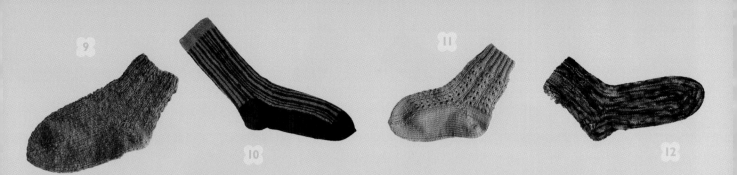

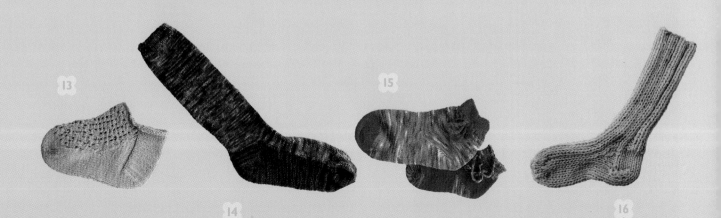

This sock is perfect for anyone who likes a bit of luxury — more boudoir glamour than bedroom slipper. Satin ribbon is threaded through eyelets for an extra touch of luxury.

Glamour Boudoir

Size
Ankle circumference 10in (25cm)
Toe to heel 8in (20.5cm)
Leg length 14½in (37cm)

Tension
36 sts and 46 rows to 4in (10cm) over st st using 2.5mm needles
Use larger or smaller needles to achieve correct tension

Materials and Equipment
- Kaalund Classic Two 100% wool (356m/388yds per 50g per 50g ball)
- 4 × 50g balls Paw Paw
- A pair of 2.5mm (UK12–13:US1–2) needles
- Set of 2.5mm (UK12–13:US1–2) double-pointed needles
- 3yds (3m) fine satin ribbon

Special techniques
- Garter stitch
- Kitchener stitch

Method

Using the pair of needles, cast on 84 sts
and work 4 rows g st.
Work lace border patt over 14 rows.

Lace border pattern

Row 1: K3, *k4, k2tog, yo, k2tog, yo, k3.
Rep from * to last 4 sts, k4.
**Row 2 and all even-numbered
rows:** K all sts.
Row 3: K3, *k2, k2tog, yo, k3, k2tog, yo,
k2. Rep from * to last 2 sts, k2.
Row 5: K2tog, yo, k1, *k1, k2tog, k5,
k2tog, yo, k1. Rep from * to last 2 sts, k2.
Row 7: K1, k2tog, yo, *k2tog, yo, k7, yo.
Rep from * to last st, k1.
Row 8 – 12: K all sts.
Row 13: K3, *k5, k2tog, yo, k4. Rep from
* to last 2 sts, k2.

Main leg

Work 152 rows in rib patt.
RS rows: K6, p1 to end.
WS rows: P6, k1 to end.

Pattern stitch for leg
and eyelets

Work 6 rows 6 x 1 rib (RS row k6, p1;
WS row p6, k1).
Next row: Rib 7, work eyelet as below,
rib to last 6 sts, make eyelet.
Rep eyelets on every 6th row.

Eyelet instructions

K2, k2 tog, yo, k2 (over 6 sts).

Shape ankle

Next row: *k2 tog, k8, rep from * 8
times, k to end (76 sts).
Divide sts and use centre 38 sts for
heel shaping.
Work 20 rows in st st on these 38 sts.

Shape heel

Row 1: K17, skpo, k1, turn.
Row 2: Sl1, p5, p2tog, p1, turn
Row 3: Sl1, k across to gap, sl1 before
the gap, k1, psso, k1, turn.
Row 4: Sl1, p across to gap, p2tog,
p1, turn.
Rep until all heel sts have been used.

Gusset

Pick up and k 19 sts along R side of heel,
k38 across instep, pick up and k 19 sts
along heel.
Arrange so there are 23 sts on N1, 30
sts on N2 and 23 sts on N3.
Next row: k6, (ssk, k6) four times, k the
rem 42 sts for sole.

Cont in rib patt as set on 34 sts at
centre top of foot and working rem 42
sts in st st for sole.
Work 6in (15cm) or length to suit foot
minus 2½in (5cm), continuing pattern on
top of foot only.
Divide sts between three needles for toe
so there are 38 on N1 for the front and
18 sts each on N2 and N3.

Shape toe

Round 1: K to last 3 sts on N1, k2tog,
k1; on N2 k1, k2tog, k to last 3 sts, k2tog,
k1; on N3 k1, k2tog, k to end.
Round 2: K all sts.
Rep these 2 rounds until 20 sts rem.

Making up

Using Kitchener stitch, graft toe sts
together.
Using fine satin ribbon, lace sock up.
Thread ribbon through eyelet holes
of top lace border and tie in a bow
as shown.

This sock is worked from the toe upwards and the leg is adorned with lace panels. Further glamour is injected by organza ribbon threaded through eyelets.

Lacy Glamour

Size

Ankle measurement 7in (18cm)
Toe to heel 8in (20.5cm)
Heel to top of leg 13in (33cm)

Tension

32 sts and 40 rows to 4in (10cm) over stocking stitch using 3mm needles.
Adjust tension as necessary/to suit chosen yarn.

Materials and Equipment

• Kaalund Yarn Expressions (462m per 100g skein)
• 2 ×100g skeins pinks
• Set of 3mm (UK11:US2) double-pointed needles
• 2m narrow organza ribbon

Special techniques

• Lace knitting
• Kitchener stitch

Toe

Cast on 6 sts on 2 needles.

Work 6 rows st st.

Using all 4 needles, pick up and k 6 sts on each of the three sides of the initial panel, then work in rounds.

Next round: *k6, inc 1, rep from * to end of round.

Cont as set until there are 48 sts (12 on each needle).

Next round: On N1 k1, m1, k12; on N2 k1, m1, k12; on N3 k1, m1, k12; on N4 k1, m1, k12.

Next round: K across.

Inc on alt rows as set by last 2 rounds, work until there are 15 sts on each needle (60 sts in all).

Work straight until foot is required length from toe to ankle.

Gusset

Separate sts thus:

N1 14 sts (foot); N2 14 sts (foot); N3 16 sts (sole); N4 16 sts (sole)

Begin working eyelets at the first gusset round. Rep on every 10th round to top of sock. Regardless of other shapings, keep 9 sts and 10 rows between eyelets.

Eyelet round: On N1 K8, k2tog, yo k4; on N2 K5, k2tog, yo k7; on N3 and N4 work as set.

Round 1: K across sts on N1 and N2; on N3 (sole sts) k1, m1, k rem sts; on N4 k to last st, m1, k1.

Round 2: K all sts.

Rep rounds 1 and 2 until there are 24 sts each on N3 and N4.

Turn heel

Slip all sts from N3 and N4 on to one needle. Work back and forth on these sts; the sts on N1 and N2 will not be worked while turning the heel.

Row 1: K27, ssk, k1, turn.

Row 2: Sl1, p7, p2tog, p1, turn.

Row 3: Sl1, k8, k2tog, p1, turn.

Row 4: Sl1, p9, p2tog, p1, turn.

Row 5: Sl1, k10, k2tog, p1, turn.

Row 6: Sl1, p11, p2tog, p1, turn.

Cont as set until all the sts have been worked and there are 28 sts on one needle. Divide sts between two needles for foot; resume working in the round.

Next 2 rounds: K.

Change to small double-pointed needles to work the lace panel up the back of the leg as you will find it easier.

Note: the round starts where N2 ends and N3 begins, and the panel is worked over the next 13 sts.

Lace panel

Round 1: K1, (yf, skpo) twice, k3, (k2tog, yf) twice, k1.

Round 2 and every alt round: k across.

Round 3: K2 (yf, skpo) twice, k1, (k2tog, yf) twice, k2.

Round 5: K3 yf, skpo, yf, sl1, k2 tog, psso, yf, k2tog, yf, k3.

Round 7: K4, yf, sl1 k2tog, psso, yf, k2 tog, yf, k4.

Round 9: K4 (k2tog, yf) twice k5.

Round 11: k3 (k2tog, yf) twice, k1, yf, skpo, k3.

Round 13: K2 (k2tog, yf) twice, k1, (yf, skpo) twice, k2.

Row 15: K1 (k2tog, yf) twice, k3, (yf, skpo) twice, k1.

Row 17: (k2tog, yf) twice, k5, (yf, skpo) twice.

Row 18: K across.

Note: the sock is being worked in the round at the same time as the lace panel is being worked, hence the reference to rounds in the instructions for the lace panel.

Leg

K9, follow lace panel of 13 sts, k38.

Round 1: Follow appropriate lace panel round.

Round 2: K across.

Rep these 2 rounds, following the correct lace panel round, until the lace panel has been worked twice.

Next 6 rounds: K across.

Rep rounds 1 and 2 above, following the correct lace panel round, until the lace panel has been worked four times.

When all four lace panels are complete work 18 rows k1, p1 rib.

Cast off loosely.

Making up

Thread ribbon through eyelet holes and tie in a bow.

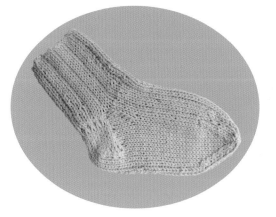

This sock is made from luxurious yarn with a touch of silk.
The heel is reinforced using slipped stitches, and the rounded
French toe is fun to work.

Silk Slouch

Size

To suit ankle circumference 10in (25.5cm)
Heel to toe 8½in (22cm) or length required

Tension

20 sts and 22 rows to 4in (10cm) in st st using 5mm needles
Use larger or smaller needles to achieve correct tension.

Materials and Equipment

- Cascade Dolce (109 yds/100m per 50g hank)
- 4 x 50g hanks 934 Buttercream
- Set of 4 x 5mm (UK6:US8) needles

Special techniques

- Raised increase
- Heel stitch
- Kitchener stitch

Leg

Cast on 48 sts divided evenly between four needles.
Join, taking care not to twist sts.
Place marker at beg of round between N1 and N4.
Work in k2, p2 rib for 2in (5cm) or length required.
Change to st st and work until sock measures desired length.

Heel flap

Row 1: To divide sts k12 (to end of N1), set 24 sts aside (12 sts on N2 and 12 sts on N3) for instep.
Turn work.
Next row: Sl1, p11 (all sts will be worked on N1 and N4).

Heel stitch

Row 1: K1, sl1 across.
Row 2: Sl1, p1 across.
Rep for about 2½in so heel flap is square.

Turn heel

Next row: Sl1, k15, skpo, k1, turn.
Next row: Sl1, p7, p2tog, p1, turn.
Next row: Sl1, k7, skpo, k1, turn.
Next row: Sl1, p to last st before gap, p2tog across gap, p1, turn.
Rep until all sts have been worked, ending on a p row.
Work in k to end of needle.

Gusset

Using N1, pick up 1 st through each sl st loop on edge of heel flap; M1 raised increase at beg of foot sts; k across foot sts; M1 raised increase at end of foot sts. Using N4, pick up 1 st through each sl st loop on edge of heel flap, k to centre of heel. Half the heel sts and the first group of picked-up gusset sts should now be on N1; half the foot sts on N2; the second half of the foot sts on N3, and the second group of gusset sts and second half of the heel sts on N4.
Next round: K to 3 sts from end of N1, k2tog, k1.

Foot

Next round: On N2 and N3 k2tog, k to 2 sts from end, k2tog; on N4 k1 ssk, k to end (at centre of heel).
Note: on this round, 4 sts are dec to remove the raised inc (M1) of the previous round from the beg and end of the foot needle. On foll rounds only 2 sts will be decreased.

Next round: K all sts.
Next and foll rounds: Dec 1 st at end of N1 and beg of N3, as above, on every other round until 48 sts rem.

Foot

Work until sock measures 6in (15cm) from back of heel or desired length. If possible, try it on: it should reach to about the beginning of the toes.

French toe

Divide sts equally between 3 needles, placing the first st of N1 exactly in the centre of foot.
Round 1: K1, sl1, k1, psso, k to last 3 sts, k2tog k1; work sts on N2 and N3 in the same way.
Round 2: K all sts.
Rep these 2 rounds until 12 sts rem.

Making up

Place sts equally on two needles and graft together using Kitchener stitch.

These cosy fun socks are made from alpaca, which is wonderful
to work with and divine to wear. Buy beautiful buttons
to fasten these sexy slouches.

Buttoned Slouch

Size

To suit ankle circumference 10in (25.5cm)
Heel to toe 7½in (19cm) adjustable
Heel to cuff 7in (18cm).

Tension

10 sts and 14 rows to 4in (10cm) over st st on
4mm needles, using yarn double throughout.
Use larger or smaller needles to achieve correct tension.

Materials and Equipment

- Garnstudio Drops Alpaca (180m per 50g)
  or any 4-ply alpaca yarn
- 4 × 50g balls
- Set of 4mm (UK8:US6) double-pointed needles
- 10 small buttons

Special techniques

- Raised increase
- Wrapped stitches
- Cables
- Kitchener grafting

Method

Using yarn double throughout, cast
on 56 sts.

Divide sts evenly between needles
(14 sts on each needle).

Work 16 rounds k.

Round 17 (cable): K sts on N1 and
N2; on N3 C4F k10, k sts on N4.

Rounds 18-22: K.

Round 23: Reverse cable by working
C4B, k all other sts.

Still using double pointed needles, begin
to work back and forth in rows.

At the same time, work a buttonhole
(see below) in every 6th row.

**Note: buttonholes will be formed
on N1 and button band on N4.**

Next row: K across sts on N1, N2 and
N3 and on N4 k10, p4 sts.

Cont as set until 39 rows have been
worked from start of sock.

Buttonhole round

K2, yo, k2tog.

Shape heel

**Note: the heel is worked using
short row shaping over the centre
28 sts, leaving the stitches not
being worked on spare needles.**

Row 1: (RS facing) k28, wrap 1, turn.

Row 2: K27, wrap 1, turn.

Rep rows 1 and 2 until 11 sts rem.

Next row: K11, pick up and k wrapped
st, replace on left needle, turn.

Next row: P11, pick up and p wrapped
st, replace on left needle, turn.

Next row: K12 pick up and k wrapped
st, replace on left needle, turn.

Next row: P12 pick up and p wrapped
st, replace on left needle, turn.

Rep as set by last 4 rows until all 28
centre sts are back on needles.

Cont on all 56 sts until 6 buttonholes
have been worked.

Work 5 rounds st st.

Rearrange sts on 3 needles ready to
return to circular knitting (14 sts on N1,
28 sts on N2, 14 sts on N3).

Next round: Cable 4 sts by transferring
first 4 sts from N1 to cable needle and
holding at front of work so they overlap
the g-st button band, k to end of round,
then k last 4 sts from N3 to N1.

Cont working in rounds until sock is 2in
(5cm) shorter than length required to toe.

Shape toe

Next round: K to last 3 sts on N1,
k2tog, k1, on N2 k1, ssk, k to end, on N3
k to last 3 sts, k2tog, k1, on N4 k1, ssk, k
to to end.

Work in rounds, cont to dec as set.

Round 6: Reverse cable by slipping 4 sts
onto cable needle and holding at back of
work, k4, complete round foll decs as set.

Cont to dec as set until 16 sts rem.

Graft sts together using Kitchener stitch.

Second sock

Complete to match first sock, reversing
cables and position of button and
buttonhole band if desired so there are
'left' and 'right' socks.

Making up

Press lightly.

Weave in any loose ends.

Sew on buttons to correspond with
buttonholes.

These beautifully cosy and comfortable socks are perfect for those times when your feet feel as though they need a hug. Just slip them on and say 'Aaah!'

'On the Edge' Alpacas

Size

To fit small (medium:large) women's sizes

Tension

30 sts and 40 rows to 10cm over st st using 3mm needles.
Use larger or smaller needles to achieve correct tension.

Materials and Equipment

- Garnstudio Drops Alpaca (180m per 50g ball) or any 3-ply yarn
- 4 × 50g balls shade 8120
- 2 × 3mm circular needles (UK11:US2–3)
- A second circular needle in the same size for grafting

Special techniques

- Using circular needles
- M1L and M1R – see abbreviations

Pattern stitches

Double garter stitch (dg-st)

Row 1: (RS) p.

Row 2: (WS) k.

Row 3: (RS) k.

Row 4: (WS) p.

Slip stitch edge

Row 1: (RS) sl1 p-wise wyif.

Row 2: (WS) k1tbl.

Right-slanting decreases

k2tog or p2tog

Left-slanting decreases

Ssk or ssp

Method

Note: Stitch markers are placed on row 1 to divide the sections of the sock. Stitch patterns for each section are established on Row 2.
Using a spare length of yarn, cast on 121 (124:125) sts.

Row 1: (WS) p38(38:37) foot sts, place foot marker; p13(14:15) heel sts, place centre heel marker; p13(13:14) heel sts, place leg marker; k41(43:43) leg sts, place cuff marker; p16 cuff sts.

Row 2: (RS) work the 16 cuff sts in dg-st, starting with row 1 (see pattern stitches); work the leg sts and heel sts in st st; work up to the last foot sts in st st; work the final st as given for the slip stitch edge beg with row 1.
Cont in the stitch patterns as set for 5 rows.

Shape heel

Row 8: Cont in patts as set, beg heel shaping by working paired dec every row thus:

RS rows: Work to 2 sts before the centre heel marker, k2tog, skpo, work to end of row.

WS rows: Work to 2 sts before centre heel marker, ssp, p2tog, work to end of row.

Repeat appropriate dec row 11 (11:12) times.

Shape calf

Next row: Work appropriate dec row and *at the same time* reposition stitch markers thus: retain the centre heel and cuff markers; remove leg and foot markers, add a centre toe marker 2 sts in

from end of the foot (the slip stitch edge stitch will be one of these 2 sts). There should now be 16 cuff sts, 41(43:43) leg sts, 2(3:3) heel sts and 38(38:37) foot sts, a total of 97(99:99)sts.

Shape toe

Row 20(21:22): Work paired inc every row thus:

RS rows: Work to 1 st before the centre toe marker, M1R, k2, M1L, work to end.

WS rows: Work to 1 st before the centre toe marker, M1L, p2, M1R, work to end.

Rep the inc row 11(12:13) more times. There should now be 13(14:15) sts between the centre toe marker and the end of the toe.

Row 31(33:35): Work as the final row of toe inc. There should now be 16 cuff sts, 42(44:47) sts between cuff and centre heel markers, 49(50:50) sts between the centre heel and centre toe markers and 14(15:16) sts from the centre toe marker to end of row, a total of 121(125:129) sts. Work 16 rows.

Complete toe shaping

Row 48(50:52): Begin working paired dec on every row thus:

RS rows: Work to 2 sts before centre toe marker, k2tog, skpo, work to end of row.

WS rows: Work to 2 sts before centre toe marker, ssp, p2tog, work to end. Rep until there are 16 cuff sts, 41(43:43) leg sts, 2 heel sts (1 on either side of the centre heel marker) and 38(38:37) foot sts, a total of 97(99:98) sts.

Row 60(63:66): Begin second half of heel shaping by working paired inc on every row thus:

RS rows: Work to 1 st before centre heel marker, M1R, k2, M1L, work to end.

WS rows: Work to 1 st before centre heel marker, M1L, p2, M1R, and work to end.

Rep the inc row 11(12:13) more times. *At the same time:*.

Row 68(72:76): Continue to work leg sts in g-st - the last row of the heel inc is row 71 (75:79). There should now be 16 sts from the beg of row to cuff marker, 54(57:58) sts between centre heel markers, 51(52:52) sts between centre heel marker and end of row, a total of 121(125:126) sts.

Work without further heel shaping until row 79(83:87).

Making up

Carefully remove the provisional cast on yarn and place the resulting loops on another circular needle. Leaving a long tail, cut the working yarn and thread the tail on a tapestry needle.

Fold sock in half, right side together, and hold the needles parallel to one another in your left hand. Working from right to left, graft the stitches together using Kitchener stitch.

Turn work inside out and locate the edge stitches along the sides of the foot and toe. Transfer to the needle, then transfer the toe edge stitches (picking up the stitches between). There should now be 20(21:22) sts. Graft these together as for main sock seam.

These extra-thick slippers are ideal for anyone who suffers from especially cold feet. Felting means that they can be made to fit the individual foot exactly.

Felted Boudoir

Size (after felting)

To fit ankle circumference 11½in (29cm)
Toe to heel 8½in (21cm) (adjustable)

Tension

26 sts and 29 rows to 4in (10cm), but not critical as work is to be felted

Materials and Equipment

- Bouton d'Or Ksar 50% baby camel, 50% pure wool (91yds per 50g)
- 4 x 50g balls in 641 Loukom
- Set of 5mm (UK6:US8) double-pointed needles
- Mesh bag for washing OR polystyrene foot last

Special techniques

- Kitchener stitch

Method

Cast on 50 sts and arrange on three needles thus: N1 12 sts; N2 25 sts; N3 13 sts.
Knit 1 row.
Knit 3 rows, foll patt on N1 and N2 and working the 25 sts on N3 in k.

Foot stitch pattern

Round 1: Yo, skpo, k2.
Round 2: K2, yo, skpo.
Round 3: K to end
Rep these 3 rows for pattern.

Shape heel

Using the 25 sts on N2, work 25 rows st st to form heel.

Turn heel

Next row: K15, skpo, k1, turn.
Next row: Sl1, p5, p2tog, turn.
Next row: Sl1, k6, skpo, k1, turn.
Next row: Sl1, p7, p2tog, turn.
Next row: Sl1, k8, skpo, k1, turn.
Next row: Sl1, p9, p2tog, turn.
Cont as set by rows above until 16 sts rem.

Shape gusset

K16 but do not turn, then pick up 16 sts along the side of the heel flap plus 1 st in the gap between the heel flap and N2 (33 sts); using N2 k the next 26 sts for the instep; with an empty needle (N3) pick up and k 1 st in the gap between the instep sts and heel flap, plus 16sts along the side of the heel flap (17 sts), then k8 sts from the heel on to N3.
Round 1: Work to 3 sts from end of N1, k2 tog k1; cont in patt across N2; on N3 k1, ssk, work to end.
Round 2: Work 1 row plain and patt as set.
Rep last 2 rounds until 50 sts rem (12 sts on N1; 13 sts on N2; 25 sts on N3).

Shape foot

Work until foot measures 2in (5cm) less than desired length and divide sts evenly between 4 needles.
Decrease round: On N1 k to last 3 sts, k2tog k1; on N2 k1, skpo, k to end; on N3 k to last 3 sts, k2tog, k1; on N4 k1 skpo, k to end.
Next round: Work straight.
Work as last 2 rounds until 32 sts rem.
Work every round as a dec round until 8 sts rem.

Making up

Using Kitchener stitch graft toe stitches together.

Felting

Place in mesh bag and put in washing machine with a non-linting towel. Set machine to boil wash. When cycle is finished remove and try on while still damp so you can shape to feet. Remove carefully and dry thoroughly. Turn tops over.

OR place slipper on a polystyrene foot last in the size required. Cover with an old nylon pop sock and tie a knot in it to fasten. Place in the washing machine as before: the sock will felt down to exactly the size of the last. Remove pop sock and leave until almost dry. Remove last and complete drying process.

These fabulous socks are playful yet warm. The beautiful colouring of the yarn is shown to advantage in the cable and lace pattern that extends over the top of the foot.

Lacy Racy Knee-highs

Size
To fit medium adult woman

Tension
24 sts and 38 rows to 4in (10cm) over stocking stitch using 3.25mm needles.

Materials and Equipment
- Colinette Jitterbug Merino (291yds/267m per 100g hank)
- 4 × 100g hanks
- Set of 3.75mm (UK9:US5) double-pointed needles
- Set of 3.50mm (UK9 – 10:US4) double-pointed needles
- Set of 3.25mm (UK10:US3) double-pointed needles
Use larger or smaller needles to achieve correct tension.

Note: two slightly different shades of this lovely variegated yarn are shown in the main images

Leg

Using 3.75mm needles, cast on 50 sts
and work 2 patt reps (16 rounds).
Change to 3.5mm needles and work
3 patt reps (24 rounds).
Change to 3.25mm needles and work
10 patt reps (80 rounds).

Cable and lace pattern

Round 1: K2, p2, k2tog, yo, p2, k4, p2
k2tog, yo, p2, k2, p1, k1, p4, k2, p2, k2tog,
yo, p2, k4, p2, k2tog, yo, p2, k2, p4.
Round 2 and all even rounds: Knit
the knit sts and purl the purl sts.
Round 3: K2, p2, yo, ssk, p2, k4, p2 yo,
ssk, p2, k2, p1, k1, p4, k2, p2, yo ssk, p2, k4,
p2, k2tog, yo, p2, k2, p4.
Round 5: As round 1.
Round 7: K2, p2, yo, ssk, p2, k4, p2,
k2tog, yo, p2, k2, p1, k1, p4, k2, p2, yo, ssk,
p2, k4, p2, yo, ssk, p2, k2, p4.
Round 8: As round 2.

Heel flap

Work 25 rows on N2 (25 sts) to
form heel.

Turn heel

Row 1: K15, skpo, k1, turn.
Row 2: Sl1, p5, p2tog, turn.
Row 3: Sl1, k6, skpo, k1, turn.
Row 4: Sl1, p7, p2tog, turn.
Row 5: Sl1, k8, skpo, k1, turn.
Row 6: Sl1, p9, p2tog, turn.
Cont as above until 16 sts rem.

Gusset

Knit stitches but do not turn. Using N1,
pick up and k 16 sts along each side of
heel flap, pick up and p1 st in the gap
between heel flap and N2 (33 sts); using
N2, k 26 sts for instep; using N3, pick up
and k1 st in the gap between instep sts
and heel flap, 16 sts along the side of the
heel flap, and 8 sts from the heel. You
should have a total of 84 sts (N1 33sts;
N2 26 sts; N3 25 sts).

Round 1: Work to 3 sts from end of
N1, k2 tog, k1; on N2, cont in cable
pattern purling the rem sts; on N3 k1,
ssk, work to end.
Round 2: Keeping cable and purl panel
correct as set, k rem sts.
Rep these 2 rounds until 50 sts rem
(12 sts on N1, 13 sts on N2 and 25 sts
on N3).

Foot

Purling top of foot and continuing cable
pattern, work until foot measures 2in
(5cm) less than length required. Divide
sts evenly between 4 needles for
dec round.
Next round: On N1 k to last 3 sts, k2
tog, k1; on N2 k1, skpo, cont in cable
pattern; on N3 k to last 2 sts, k2tog, k1;
on N4 k1, skpo, k to end.
Work as above, alternating dec/non-dec
rounds until 32 sts rem.
Work every round as a dec round until
8 sts rem.

Making up

Graft stitches together using Kitchener
stitch.
Press lightly.

This sock is specially designed to wear with clogs.
The cable patterning at the back of the heel adds a fashionable
touch where it will show!

Cable Clog

Size

To fit ankle circumference 9in (23cm)
Heel to toe 9in (23cm)

Tension

20 sts and 28 rows to 4in (10cm) measured over
st st using 4mm needles.

Materials and Equipment

- Cygnet DK 100% merino wool (104m per 50g ball)
- 3 x 50g balls 2134 Rose Pink
- Set of 4mm (UK8:US6) double-pointed needles.
- Cable needle

Special techniques

- Cable patterning
- Kitchener graft
- Short row shaping

Cable pattern

Work 6 rows.

Round 7: Work C3F (slip next 3 sts on to a cable needle and hold at front of work; k next 3 sts, k3 from cable needle) in position as given.

Round 8: Work 1 row.

These 8 rows form cable patt at back of heel and are rep as required.

Method

Cast on 40 sts divided evenly between four needles.

Round 1: P2, k8 across N1; p2, k8 across N2; p2, k8 across N3; p2, k8 across N4.

Rep last round 6 times.

Round 7: Work sts on N1, N2, and N3 as before; on N4 p2, C3F, p2.

Round 8: Work 1 row.

Rep last 8 rows to end of heel flap.

Divide sts so there are 20 sts on N1, 10 sts on N2 and 10 sts on N3.

Work 22 heel rows for beg of heel flap, slipping the first st on every row and keeping cable patt correct.

Heel (short row shaping)

Next row: K13, ssk, k1, turn.

Next row: Sl1, p6, p2tog, turn.

Next row: Sl1, k to 1 st before gap produced on previous row, ssk, turn.

Next row: Sl1, p to first st before gap, p2tog, turn.

Rep last 2 rows until all heel sts have been worked.

Stop cable patt now, but cont with centre rib panel as set at centre top of foot until toe.

Shape gusset

Round 1: On N1, K14 heel sts, then pick up and k 12 sts along heel flap; k22 instep sts on N2; on N3 pick up 12 sts from other side of heel then knit the first 7 sts from N1 to arrive at centre of heel sts (60 sts).

Round 2: K to last 3 sts on N1, k2 tog, k1; k22 on N2; on N3 k1, ss4, k to last 2 sts, k2tog.

Round 3: K.

Repeat rounds 2 and 3 until 44 sts rem.

Foot

Work straight until foot measures 2in (5cm) less than length required.

Shape toe

Round 1: K to last 3 sts on N1, k2tog, k1; on N2 k1, ssk, k to last 3sts, k2 tog, k1; on N3 k1, ssk, k to end.

Round 2: K.

Rep rounds 1 and 2 until 20 sts rem.

Rep round 1 until 8 sts rem.

Making up

Using Kitchener stitch, graft rem toe sts together.

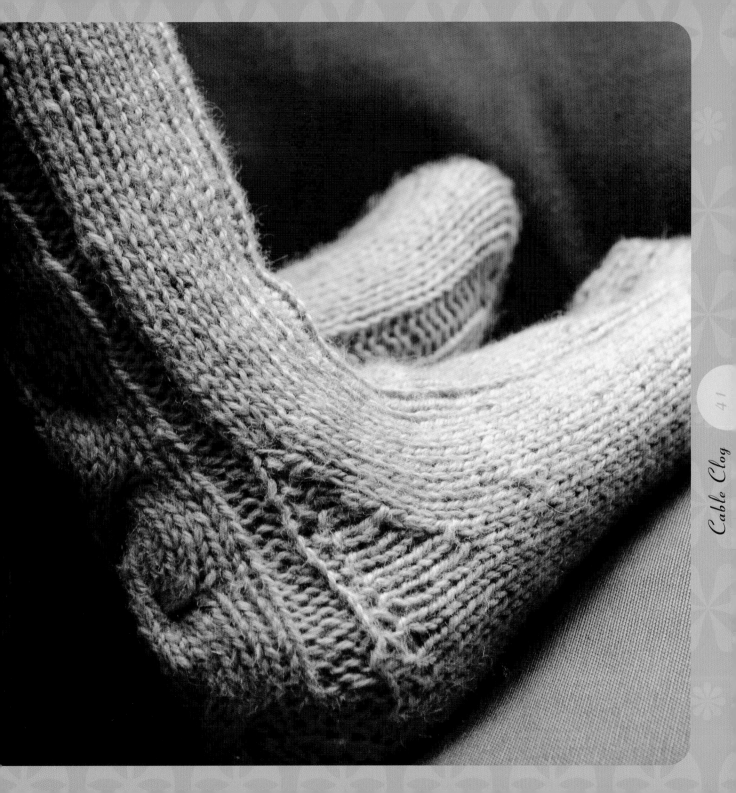

These socks are great to make for the guy who deserves
a touch of luxury. Handspun cashmere is wonderful
to work with, and even nicer to wear.

Cashmere Slouch

Size
Ankle circumference 8½in (21.5cm)
Toe to heel 9½in (24cm)

Tension
18–19 sts and 26 rows to 4in (10cm) in st st using 4mm
needles
Use larger or smaller needles to achieve correct tension.

Materials and Equipment
- Teo hand-spun cashmere (see note overleaf)
- 200g brown
- 1 set of 4mm (UK8:US6) double-pointed needles

Special techniques
- Short row shaping (for heel)
- Kitchener stitch
- Wrapped stitches (see abbreviations)

Note: the yarn used for these socks is hand-spun cashmere from the Isle of Skye and the thickness may vary. Check your tension carefully, or substitute yarn of approximately Aran weight

Method

Cast on 44 sts and distribute evenly between three needles.
Join taking care not to twist sts.
Work in k1, p1 rib for 5 rows.
Change to k3, p1 rib and work 20 rows.
Cont in st st throughout.

Shape heel

Row 1: With RS facing k19, wrap 1, turn (20 sts).
Row 2: P19, wrap 1, turn.
Rep rows 1 and 2, working 1 st fewer every 2 rows until 11 sts rem on needle.
Next row: K11, pick up and k wrapped st, replace on LH needle, turn.
Next row: P11, pick up and p wrapped st, replace on LH needle, turn.
Next row: K12, pick up and k wrapped st, replace on LH needle, turn.
Next row: P12, pick up and p wrapped st, replace on LH needle, turn.
Rep these rows until all 44 sts are back on needles.
Work straight until sock is 2in (5cm) shorter than required length.
Divide sts evenly between four needles for toe shaping.

Shape toe

Next round: On N1, k to last 3 sts, k2tog, k1; on N2, k1, skpo, k to end; on N3, k to last 3 sts, k2tog, k1; on N4, k1, skpo, k to end (dec round).
Next round: K to end.
Work as above alternating dec/non-dec rounds until 32 sts rem.
Work every round as a dec round until 8 sts remain.

Making up

Using Kitchener stitch graft toe sts together.
Press lightly.
Hand wash only and dry flat.

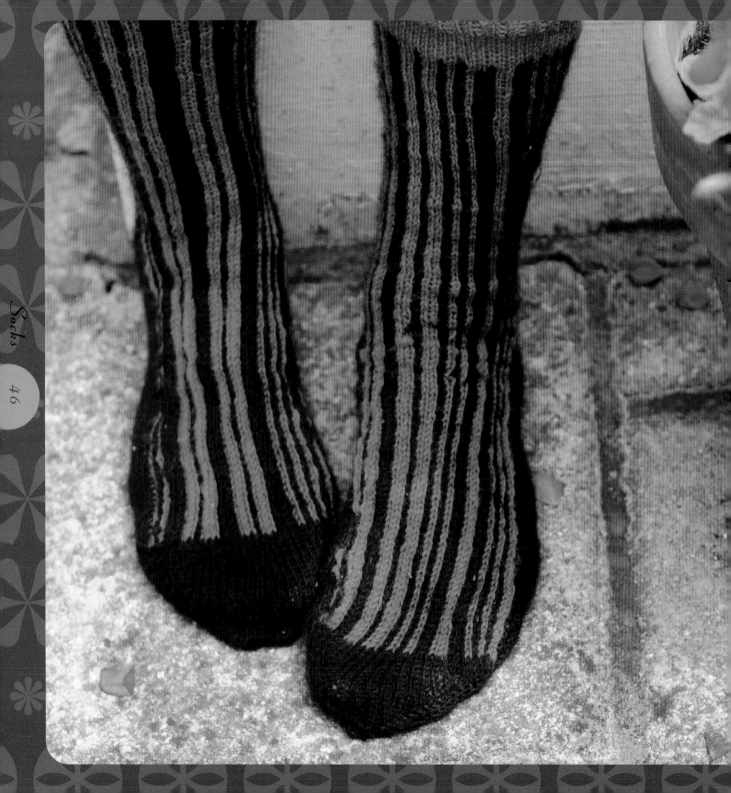

These colourful socks add a touch of fun to a sober business suit and can be worked in his favourite shades. They have a comfortable rounded toe and the heel is great to work.

City Stripe

Size

To fit ankle circumference 8½in (22cm) mf
Heel to toe 9in (23cm).

Tension

32 sts to 10cm measured over Fair Isle pattern using 3mm needles.

Materials and Equipment

- Cygnet 4 ply 75% wool/ 25% nylon (205m per 50g ball)
- 2 x 50g balls Black (M)
- 2 x 50g balls Fuchsia (C)
- Set of 3mm (UK11:US2–3) double-pointed needles

Special techniques

Fair Isle

Method

Using M, cast on 64 sts divided between 3 needles (21 sts on N1; 21 sts on N2; 22 sts on N3).

Join, taking care not to twist sts.

Work 5 rounds k1, p1 rib.

Work 7 rounds k.

Join in C and work in colour patt throughout (see chart).

Work straight in patt until leg measures 4½in (11.5cm).

Divide stitches so there are 32 sts on heel needle and 16 sts on each instep needle.

Shape heel

Work on 32 heel sts in M only and in st st for 3 in (7.5cm) ending with a purl row.

Next row: K18, skpo, turn.

Next row: Sl1, p4, p2tog, turn.

Next row: Sl1, k5, skpo, turn.

Next row: Sl1, p6, p2tog, turn.

Cont in this way, working 1 st more on every row until there are 18 sts being worked on the needle.

Next row: k18, pick up 15 sts along side of heel; work across instep needle; using N3 pick up 15 sts along side of heel; k9 from the heel needle onto this needle. There should now be 24 sts on each heel needle and 32 sts on the instep needle.

Next round: Working from division in centre of heel, work to last 3 sts on next needle, k2 tog, k1, work across instep, on N3 k1, skpo, work to end of needle.

Next round: Work, keeping upper foot patt correct as set.

Rep these last 2 rounds until there are 16 sts on each heel needle.

Working sole in 2 x 2 Fair Isle (see chart) and upper foot in Fair Isle as set, work straight until foot measures 8½in (21.5cm) from back of heel (allowing 2½in (6.5cm) for toe).

Shape toe

Round 1: Using M, on N1 k to last 3 sts, k2 tog, k1; on instep needle, k1, skpo, k to last 3 sts, k2 tog, k1; on N3 k1, skpo, k to end of needle.

Round 2: Using M, k.

Rep these 2 rounds until 16 sts rem.

Making up

Graft rem sts together.

City Stripe chart
64 sts x 9 rows

■ M ☐ C

**repeat these 4 sts
for sole after heel shaped**

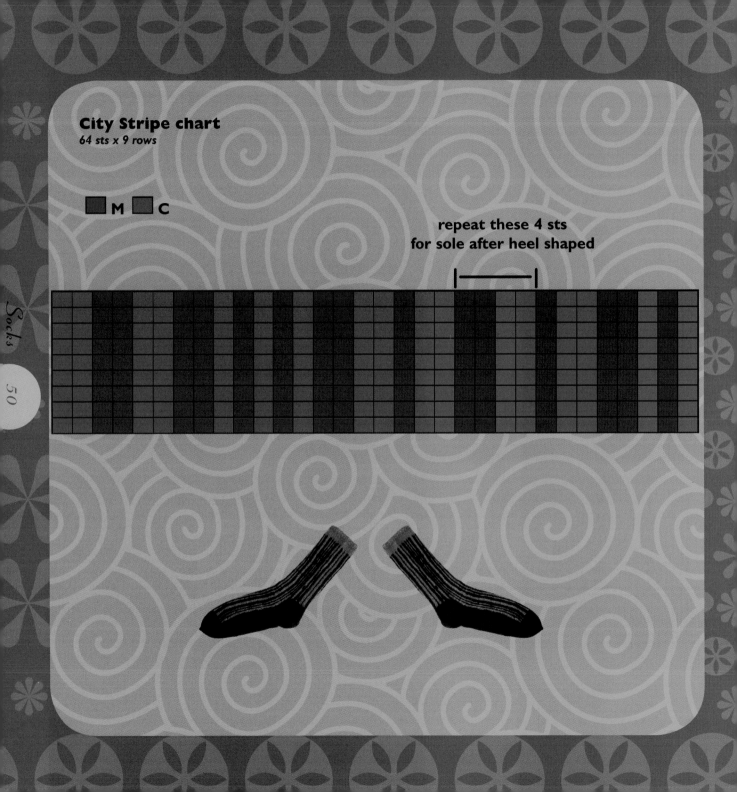

| centre front of sock

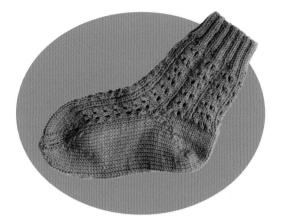

This sock is particularly good for anyone with wide feet.
The lovely lacy pattern is designed to flatter the foot.

Fancy Feet

Size

To suit ankle circumference 8in (20cm)
Heel to toe length (adjustable) 10in (25cm).

Tension

Not critical as lace rib pattern is stretchy.

Materials and Equipment

- Cygnet Chunky 75% wool, 25% polyamide (148m per 100g)
- 3 × 100g balls in 2184 Petrol
- Set of 3.25mm (UK10:US3) double-pointed needles

Special techniques

- wyif = with yarn in front
- wyib = with yarn at back
- Kitchener stitch

Method

Cast on 56 sts divided evenly between four needles and work 14 rows k2, p2 rib.

Work in eyelet rib pattern (see below) for 24 rounds.

Set aside 28 sts and work heel back and forth on rem 28 sts.

Eyelet rib pattern

Rounds 1 and 2: *K1, p1, k5, p1, rep from * to end.

Row 3: *K1, p1, k2tog, yo, k1, yo, ssk, rep from * to end.

Row 4: *K1, p1, k5, p1, rep from * to end.

Heel

Next row: K29, sl1 wyif, turn.
Next row: Sl1 wyif, p28, sl1 wyib, turn.
Next row: Sl1 wyib, k27 sl1 wyif, slip same stitch back, turn.
Next row: P26, sl1 wyib.
Next row: K25, sl1 wyif.
Next row: P24, sl1 wyib.
Next row: K23, sl1 wyif.
Next row: P22, sl1 wyib.
Cont as set until there are 'wrapped' sts either side of 14 'live' sts.

Picking up wrapped stitches

Row 1: Work across the 14 'live' sts to the first unworked wrapped st; pick up both wrap and st and k tog; wrap the next st (so it has 2 wraps); turn.

Row 2: Slip the first double wrapped st; p across to the first unworked wrapped st; pick up both wrap and st and p tog; wrap the next st as before; turn.
Repeat, picking up both wrap and stitch and working together as set, until there are 28 sts again.

Foot

Divide the foot sts between N1 and N2 and the heel sts between N3 and N4. Resume working in the round, working top of foot in eyelet pattern on N1 and N2 and sole in st st on N3 and N4, until work measures approx 2½in (6.5cm) less than length required.

Shape toe

Round 1: On N1 k to last 3 sts, k2tog, k1; on N2 k1, k2tog, p to last 3 sts, k2tog, k1; on N3 k1, k2tog, k to end.
Round 2: K.
Rep these rounds until 20 and 24 sts remain respectively.

Making up

Graft rem sts together using Kitchener stitch.

These easy-to-make, innovative socks are worked sideways using a circular needle. Pretty buttons are a fun way to fasten the flaps.

'On the Edge' Dance

Size

To suit: small (medium: large) women's sizes

Tension

30 sts and 40 rows to 4in (10cm) in st st using 3.25mm needles

Use larger or smaller needles to achieve correct tension.

Materials and Equipment

- Colinette Jitterbug 100% Merino Wool (267m per 100g)
- 2 × 100g hanks Fruit Coulis
- Pair of 3.25mm (UK10:US3) needles
- 2 × 3.25mm (UK10:US3) circular needles
- 6 buttons

Special techniques

- Use of circular needles
- Raised increase
- Heel stitch
- Kitchener stitch
- MIL and MIR – see abbreviations

Note: The socks are worked back and forth using a circular needle, which provides the flexibility to take the curve of the heel and toe. A second circular needle is used for grafting.

Leg and foot

Using a provisional cast-on method, cast on 97(98:99) sts. On the first row, markers are placed to divide the sections of the sock, and on the second row the stitch patterns used for each section are established.

Row 1: (WS) p38(38:37) foot sts, place foot marker; p13(14:15) heel sts, place centre heel marker; p13(13:14) heel sts, place leg marker; k8(8:8) leg sts, place cuff marker; p25 cuff sts.

Row 2: (RS) work the 25 cuff sts in d-g st (see below; beg with row 1), work the leg and heel sts and up to the last foot sts in st st; work the edge stitch in the slip stitch edge patt (see below; beg with row 1).

Work in the stitch patts as set for 5 further rows.

Double garter stitch (dg-st)

Row 1: (RS) Purl.
Row 2: (WS) Knit.
Row 3: (RS) Knit.
Row 4: (WS) Purl.

Slip stitch edge

Row 1: (RS) Sl 1 st p-wise with yarn in front.
Row 2: (WS) K1 tbl.

Shape heel

Row 8: Cont in the stitch patts as set, and *at the same time*, begin the heel shaping by working paired dec every row thus:

RS rows: Work to 2 sts before the centre heel marker, k2tog, skpo, k to end.
WS rows: Work to 2 sts before centre heel marker, ssp, p2tog, work to end.
Rep appropriate dec rows 11 (12:13) times.
Keep the centre heel and cuff markers, and add a centre toe marker 2 sts in from end of the foot (the slip st edge st counts as one of these sts).

Shape toe

Row 20 (21:21): Begin working paired inc every row thus:
RS rows: Work to 1 st before the centre toe marker, M1R, k2, M1L, work to end.
WS rows: Work to 1 st before the centre toe marker, M1L, p2, M1R, work to end.
Rep the inc row until there are 13(15:16) sts between the centre toe marker and the end of the toe, which should be row 31(33:35).
Work 16 rows without increasing.
Row 48(50:52): cBegin working paired dec on every row thus:

RS rows: Work to 2 sts before the centre toe marker, k2tog, skpo, work to end.
WS rows: Work to 2 sts before centre toe marker, ssp, p2tog, work to end.
Rep the dec row 11(12:13) more times.

Shape heel

Row 60(63:66): Begin second half of heel shaping by working paired inc every row thus:
RS rows: Work to 1 st before centre heel marker, M1R, k2, M1L, work to end.
WS rows: Work to 1 st before centre heel marker, M1L, p2, M1R, and work to end.
Rep the inc row 11(12:13) more times.
Work straight ending with row 79(83:91).

Shape cuff overlap

Work 16 rows on cuff sts only.
Cast off 16 cuff sts at either side.

Making up

Remove the provisional cast on and place the resulting 'live' loops on the second circular needle.
Cut the working yarn, leaving a long tail, and thread this on a tapestry needle.
Fold sock in half, RS together, and place needles parallel to one another.
Holding the needles in your left hand and working right to left, graft the two sides together using Kitchener stitch.
Fold flap over and attach buttons through both flap pieces at the back of the heel.

These dainty socks are made to a very similar pattern to the felted boudoir socks (see page 31) but using smaller needles.

Comfort Boudoir

Size

To fit ankle circumference 10in (26cm)
Toe to heel 8.5in (21cm) (adjustable)

Tension

26 sts and 34 rows to 4in (10cm) over stocking stitch using 3mm needles

Materials and Equipment

- Bouton d'Or Ksar 50% baby camel, 50% pure wool (91yds per 50g)
- 3 x 50g balls 641 Loukom
- Set of 3mm (UK11:US2–3) double-pointed needles

Special techniques

- Kitchener stitch

Leg

Cast on 50 sts and arrange on three needles so there are 12 sts on N1, 26 sts on N2 and 12 sts on N3.
Knit 1 row.
Knit 3 rows, foll patt on N1 and N2 and working the 26 sts on N3 in k.

Foot stitch pattern

Round 1: Yo, skpo, k2.
Round 2: K2, yo, skpo.
Round 3: K.
Rep these 3 rows for pattern.

Shape heel

Using the 26 sts on N2, work 25 rows st st to form heel.

Turn heel

Next row: K15, skpo, k1, turn.
Next row: Sl1, p5, p2tog, p1 turn.
Next row: Sl1, k6, skpo, k1, turn.
Next row: Sl1, p7, p2tog, p1 turn.
Next row: Sl1, k8, skpo, k1, turn.
Next row: Sl1, p9, p2tog, p1 turn.
Cont as set by rows above until 16 sts rem on needle.

Shape gusset

K16 but do not turn, then pick up 16 sts along the side of the heel flap plus 1 st in the gap between the heel flap and N2 (33 sts); using N2, work the next 24 patt

sts for the instep; with an empty needle (N3) pick up and k1 in the gap between the instep sts and heel flap, plus 16 sts along the side of the heel flap (17sts), k8 sts from the heel onto N3.

Round 1: Work to 3 sts from end of N1, k2 tog k1; cont in patt across N2; on N3 k1, ssk, work to end.
Round 2: Work 1 row plain and patt.
Rep last 2 rounds until 50 sts rem (13 sts on N1; 24 sts on N2; 13 sts on N3).
25 sts on N1, 24 patt sts on N2; 25 sts on N3.

Shape foot

Work until foot measures 2in (5cm) less than desired length. Divide sts between 4 needles so there are 13 sts on N1; 12sts

on N2; 12 sts and 13 sts on N4.
Next round: K10, k2 tog, k1 on N1; k across sts on N2 and N3; on N4 ssk, k10 (48 sts). This removes the extra 2 sts allowing you to decrease evenly for the foot.
Decrease round: On N1 k to last 3 sts, k2tog k1; on N2 k1,ssk, k to end; on N3 k to last 3 sts, k2tog, k1; on N4 k1 ssk, k to end (44 sts).
Next round: Work straight.
Rep as last 2 rounds until 32 sts rem.
Work every round as a dec round until 8 sts rem.

To make up

Using Kitchener stitch, graft toe stitches together.

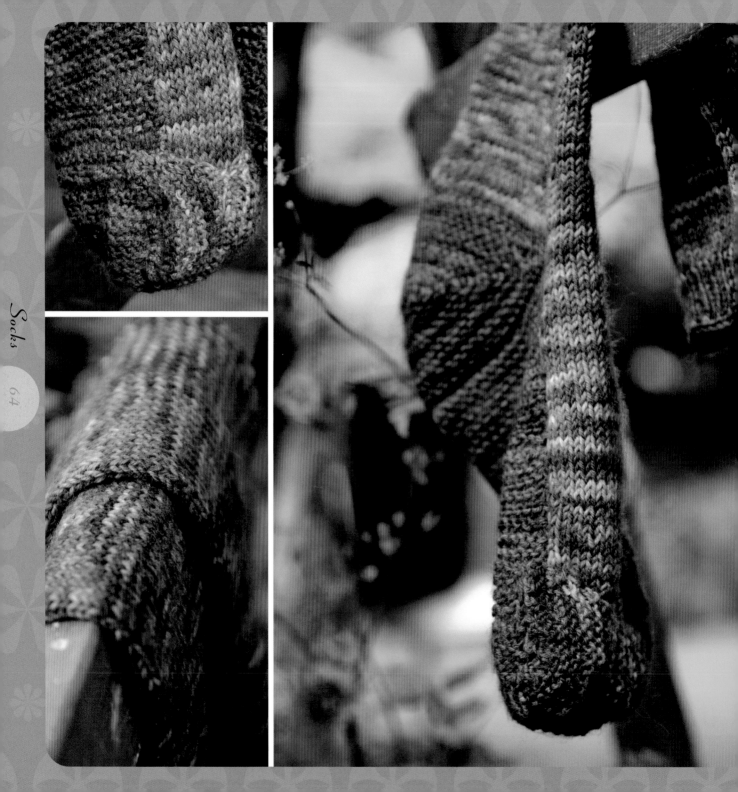

Fabulous for wearing round the house, these look just like shoes and socks! If you do not fancy the bow, instructions are given for an alternative frilled trim.

Trendy Shoesocks

Size
Ankle circumference 8in (20.5cm)
Toe to heel 9in (23cm)

Tension
24 sts and 28 rows to 4in (10cm) over stocking stitch using 3.25mm needles
Use larger or smaller needles to achieve correct tension.

Materials and Equipment
- Araucania Ranco 75% wool, 25% nylon (376yds per 100g skein)
- 1 x 100g skein 483 (M)
- 1 x 100g skein multi 502 (C)
- Set of 3.25mm (UK10:US3) double-pointed needles

Special techniques
- Wrapped stitches (see techniques)
- The sock is worked from the toe up

Toe

Cast on 8 sts and work 6 rows st st to form a rectangle.

Turn so that WS of work is facing.

Round 1: Using N1, k8 along working edge of rectangle; using N2 pick up and k6 from next side; using N3 pick up and k8 from next side; using N4 pick up and k6 from final edge. Work in g-st thus:

Round 2: K8, m1 on N1; k6, m1 on N2; k8, m1 on N3; k6, m1 on N4 (32 sts).

Round 3: K9, m1 on N1; k7 on N2; k9, m1 on N3; k7 on N4 (34 sts).

Round 4: K10, m1 on N1; k7, m1 on N2; k10, m1 on N3; k7, m1 on N4 (38 sts).

Round 5: K11, m1 on N1; k8 on N2; k11, m1 on N3; k8 on N4 (40 sts).

Round 6: K12, m1 on N1; k8, m1 on N2; k12, m1 on N3; k8, m1 on N4 (44 sts).

Round 7: K13, m1 on N1; k9, m1 on N2; k13, m1 on N3; k9, m1 on N4 (48 sts).

Round 8: K14, m1 on N1; k10 on N2; k14, m1 on N3; k10 on N4 (50 sts).

Round 9: K15, m1 on N1; k10 on N2; k15, m1 on N3; k10 on N4 (52 sts).

Round 10: K16, m1 on N1; k10, m1 on N2; k16, m1 on N3; k10, m1 on N4 (56 sts).

Round 11: K17, m1 on N1; k11, m1 on N2; k17, m1 on N3; k11, m1 on N4 (60 sts).

Round 12: K18 on N1; k12 on N2; k18 on N3; k12 on N4 (60 sts).

Foot

Next round: On N1 g-st in M; on N2 g-st in M; on N3 st st in C; on N4 g-st in M.

Cont in this way for 50 rows (or to length required).

Heel

With RS facing and using C, begin short row shaping using sts on N1, N2 and N4 (42 sts)

Row 1: K19, wrap 1, turn.

Row 2: P19 wrap 1, turn.

Rep rows 1 and 2 until 14 sts remain.

Next row: K14, pick up and k wrapped st, replace on L needle, turn.

Next row: P14, pick up and p wrapped st, replace on L needle, turn.

Next row: K15, pick up and k wrapped st, replace on L needle, turn.

Next row: P15, pick up and p wrapped st, replace on L needle, turn.

Rep these rows until all stitches are back on the needles.

Divide sts between three needles and resume working in the round.

Work 38 rounds (or length required).

Work 8 further rounds for a sock with a bow OR work alternative frilled top (see below).

Bow

Cast on 18 sts and k 14 rows.

Cast off.

Alternative frilled top (no bow)

Next round: K all 60 sts

Next round: *K1, m1, rep from * to end. (120 sts).

Work 3 rounds st st.

Next round: *K1 m1, rep from * to end. (240 sts).

Work 2 rounds st st.

Cast off.

Making up

Fold bow piece ends to middle.

Place seam downwards and attach to front of sock to form a bow.

Darn in ends.

No need to worry about lost socks with this design
– just work three in coordinating shades.
They are great fun, and ideal for children.

Pair and a Spare

Size

To fit ankle circumference 8in (20cm)
Heel to toe length 7in (18cm)

Tension

30 sts and 42 rows to 4in (10cm) on 2.5mm needles

Materials and Equipment

- Cygnet 4-ply 75% wool, 25% nylon (205m per 50g)
- 2 x 50g balls red (M)
- Regia multi sock yarn 75% wool, 25% polyamide
  (210m per 50g ball)
- 2 x 50g balls orange/blue/yellow (C)
- Set of 2.5mm (UK13:US1) double-pointed needles

Special techniques

- Kitchener stitch
- Easy heel

Basic sock

Cast on 64 sts divided so there are 32 sts on N1, 16 sts on N2 and 16 sts on N3. Using M, work 15 rounds k1, p1 rib.

Next round: * K4, yo, k2 tog, rep from * to end for eyelets.

Change to C and work 4 rounds st st. Check that there are 32 sts on N1 for top of foot; 16 on N2 and 16 on N3.

Note: The sts on N2 and N3 form the heel; inc points are where N2 and N3 meet either end of N1.

Easy heel

Inc round: K sts on N1; inc 1, k sts on N2, k to last st on N3, inc 1.

Next and every alternate round: K all sts.

Rep until there are 32 sts on N1, 30 sts on N2 and 30 sts on N3.

Decrease round: K across 32 sts on N1, then k2tog, k1 from N2 onto N1, turn.

Next row: Sl1, p to end, then p2tog, p1 using 3 sts from next needle, turn.

Next row: Sl1, k to end of needle; from next needle k2tog, k1, turn.

Next row: Sl1, k to end of needle; from next needle k2tog, k1 turn.

Next row: Sl1, p to end; from next needle p2 tog, p1.

Work as set until there are 16 sts on N1, 30 sts on N2 and 30 sts on N3.

Foot

Work 35 rounds C.

Toe

Round 1: Using M, k to 2 sts from end of N1, sl2 k-wise, k1 from N2 and pass slipped sts over; work across N2 to last 2 sts, sl2 k-wise, k1 from N3 and pass slipped sts over.

Round 2: K all sts.

Rep last 2 rounds until 12 sts rem across all needles.

Variation 1

Using C, cast on 64 sts and work 13 rounds k1, p1 rib.

Change to M and work 2 rounds k.

Next round: * K4, yo, k2 tog, rep from * to end for eyelets.

Next round: K all sts using M.

Next round: Change to C and k all sts. Work 3 rows C.

Heel increases

Work as for basic sock.

Knit 35 rounds C.

Change to M for toe.

Toe

Round 1: K to 2 sts from end of N1, sl2 k-wise, k1 from N2 and psso the k1, work across N2 to last 2 sts, sl2 k-wise, k1 from N3 and psso the k1.

Round 2: K all sts.

Rep last 2 rounds until 12 sts rem across all needles.

Variation 2

Using C, work 15 rounds k1, p1 rib.

Next round: * K4, yo, k2 tog, rep from * to end for eyelets.

Work 1 round C, 7 rounds M, 4 rounds C, 3 rounds M, 7 rounds C.

Next round: *K2M, k2C, rep from * to end.

Heel increases

Work as for basic sock using M.

Foot

Work 3 rounds C, 2 rounds M and 3 rounds C.

Next round: *K2C, k2M, rep from * to end.

Rep last round twice more.

Next round: *K2M, k2C, rep from * to end.

Rep last round twice more.

Work 4 rounds C in g-st.

Work 3 rounds M.

Next round: *K2M, k2C, rep from * to end.

Rep last round 3 times more.

Work 3 rounds C, 10 rounds M, 1 round C.

Toe

Shape as for basic sock using C.

Making up

Cut the yarn and graft sts tog using Kitchener stitch.

This young, fun design is just right for relaxing at home. The yarn is used double throughout for extra snugness.

Size

To suit UK size 4–5 (5–6:6–7)
Foot length 8½(9½/10½)in (22(24:27)cm)

Tension

11 sts and 15 rows to 4in (10cm) over patt
on 7mm needles, using yarn double throughout.
Use larger or smaller needles to achieve correct tension.

Materials and Equipment

• Cygnet Aran, 75% British wool and 25% polyamide
  (224m per 100g).
• 3 x 100g balls 233 Lavender
• Set of 7mm (UK2:US10.5) double-pointed needles

Special techniques

• M1
• Kitchener stitch

Leg

Cast on 28(30:32) sts divided evenly between 4 needles.
Join, taking care not to twist sts.

Size 4-5 only: K1, *p2, k2 rep from * to last 3 sts, p2, k1. Rep until work measures 10in (26cm).

Size 5-6 only: K1, p3 *p2, k2, rep from * to last 4 sts, p3, k1.
Rep until sock measures 5in (12cm), then dec 1 st in each p3 section (28 sts).
Next round: K1, p2 *p2, k2, rep from * to last 4 sts, p2, k1.
Cont until work measures 10½in (26cm).

Size 6-7 only: K1, p4, *p2, k2, rep from * to last 7 sts, k2, p4, k1. Rep until sock measures 5½in (14cm), then dec 1 st in each p4 section (30 sts).
Next round: K1, p3 *p2, k2, rep from * to last 4 sts, p3, k1. Cont until work measures 11in (28cm), then dec 1 st in each p3 section.
Next round: K1, p3 *p2, k2, rep from * to last 4 sts, p3, k1.
Cont until work measures 12in (30cm).

Divide for heel (all sizes)

Set aside 14 sts (7 sts on either side) for gusset and work back on the rem 14 sts for heel for 2(2½:3)in or 5(6:7)cm. Place marking thread here.

Decrease for heel

Row 1: K until 5(6:6)sts left on row, k2tog turn.
Row 2: P until 5(6:7)sts left on row, p2tog turn.
Row 3: K until 4(5:5)sts left on row, k2tog, turn.
Row 4: P until 4(5:5)sts left on row, p2tog turn.
Cont in this way, leaving one st fewer before each dec, until 6(7:8)sts rem.

Foot

Pick up 7(9:10) sts on each side of heel. Arrange all 34 (38:42) sts, including those set aside, on double-pointed needles.
Next round: Work the centre 16 sts in rib and the rest in st st.
Next round: Work in st st and rib but dec by working k2tog into the back of the 2 sts before the rib and working the 2 sts after the rib as k2 tog.
Rep last 2 rounds until 24(26:28) sts rem.
Work straight until foot measures approx 7(8:8½)in or 18 (20:22)cm from heel.
Insert a marker thread on each side 12(13:14) sts between each marker.

Decrease for toe

Cont in st st on all sts, dec on either side of each marker thread (MT) thus:
Next round: K2tog, k1, MT, k1, k2tog into back of st.
Next round: Work in st st.
Rep the last 2 rows a total of 3 times
Dec on every row 1(1:2) times (8:10:8) sts.

Making up

Using Kitchener stitch graft sts together.

These socks are ideal for visits to the gym. They are comfortable
to wear and the 'go-faster' stripe pattern adds interest.

Go-faster Sport

Size

To fit shoe sizes 5–6 (7–8:9–10:11–12)

Tension

28 sts and 32 rows to 4in (10cm) over stocking stitch
using 2.75mm needles
Use larger or smaller needles to achieve correct tension.

Materials and Equipment

- 4-ply cotton yarn
- 2 x 50g balls white (M)
- Oddment (approx 15–25g) contrast (C)
- Set of 2.75mm (UK12:US2) double-pointed needles

Special techniques

- Garter stitch in the round (k 1 row, p 1 row)

Ankle

Cast on 44(48:52:56) sts loosely and join, taking care not to twist sts.

Place a marker between first and second sts to indicate beg of round.

Divide the sts so there are 14(16:18:20) on N1, 16 (18:20:22) on N2 and 14(16:18:20) sts on N3.

Next round: K14(16:18:20) sts on N1; k16 (18:20:22) sts on N2, turn.

Next row: P across all sts, turn.

Next row: K across all sts, turn.

Next row: P across all sts, turn.

Next row: K across 14(16:18:20) sts on N3.

Work 2 rounds.

Next round: Work across in M, but on N2 work 6 sts 6M, 10 sts C, 6 sts M. Rep this round 4 times.

Work 18(20:24:24) rounds st st st.

Heel flap

Rearrange sts so there are 11(12:13:14) on N1, 22(24:26:28) on N2 and 11 (12:13:14) on N3.

Next row: K33(36:39:42), turn.

Work sts on N2 back and forth in patt (see below) for 22(24:26:28) rows.

Heel pattern

Row 1: Using C, k1, sl1 along the row.

Row 2: Using C, purl.

Row 3: Using C, k1, sl1 along the row.

Row 4: Using M, purl.

Row 5: Using M, k1, sl1 along the row.

Row 6: Using M, purl.

Row 7: Using M, k1, sl1 along the row.

Row 8: Using M, k1, sl1 along the row.

Row 9: Using M, purl.

Row 10: Using C, k1, sl1 along the row.

Row 11: Using C, purl.

Row 12: Using C, k1, sl1 along the row.

Row 13: Using M, purl.

Row 14: Using M, k1, sl1 along the row.

Row 15: Using M, purl.

Row 16: Using M, k1, sl1 along the row.

Row 17: Using M, purl.

Row 18: Using M, k1, sl1 along the row.

Row 19: Using C, purl.

Row 20: Using C, k1, sl1 along the row.

Row 21: Using C, purl.

Row 22: Using M, k1, sl1 along the row.

Row 23: Using C, purl.

Row 24: Using M, k1, sl1 along the row.

Row 25: Using C, purl.

Row 26: Using C, k1, sl1 along the row.

Row 27: Using C, purl.

Row 28: Using C, k1, sl1 along the row.

Row 29: Using C, purl.

Row 30: Using M, k1, sl1 along the row.

Turn heel

Row 1: K1, skpo, k to last 7 sts, k2tog, k5.

Row 2 and foll alt rows: K all sts.

Rep these 2 rows until 14(14:16:16) sts rem on N2 finishing with row 2.

Instep (top foot and sole)

With the spare needle, pick up 14(15:16:17) sts along the edge of the heel flap, picking up from the knit rows for a clean finish. Knit sts on N3 and N1. Pick up 13(14:15:16) sts on the edge of the heel flap, picking up from the knit rows to ensure a clean finish, then k to end of round 64(68:74:78) sts.

Rearrange sts so there are 21(22:24:25) sts on N1, 22(24:26:28) sts on N2 and 21(22:24:25) sts on N3.

Instep decrease

Round 1: K to last 3 sts on N1, k2tog, k1; k all sts on N2; on N3 k1, skpo, k rem sts.

Rep last round 9(9:11:11) times 44(48:52:56) sts.

Rearrange sts so there are 11 (12:13:14) sts on N1, 22 (24:26:28) sts on N2 and 11 (12:13:14) sts on N3.

Foot

Work 32(36:40:44) rounds in st st.

Shape toe

Round 1: P to last 3 sts on N1, p2tog, p1; on N2 p1, p2tog, p to last 3 sts, p2tog, p1; on N3 p1, p2tog, p rem sts.

Round 2: K all sts.

Rep these 2 rounds until 20(20:20:24) sts rem, finishing with round 2.

Making up

Cast off using the three needle cast-off (see techniques) or graft stitches tog.

The spiralling pattern is simple and great fun to work.
The knitted fabric is so flexible that the socks can be made
without a heel yet still fit perfectly.

Spiral Clog

Size

To suit ankle circumference 10in (25.5cm)

Tension

18 sts and 23 rows to 4in (10cm) in st st using
2.75/3mm needles.
Use larger or smaller needles to achieve correct tension.

Materials and Equipment

- Hand-dyed 4-ply
- 4 x 50g balls dark grey
- Set of 2.75mm or 3mm (UK11–12/US2–3)
  double-pointed needles

Special techniques

- Spiral rib
- Kitchener stitch

Tip

Use a yarn that produces about 12.5 wraps per inch – see note in techniques section for advice on yarn substitution.

Leg

Cast on 66 sts divided evenly between 4 needles.
Join, taking care not to twist sts.
Work in k3, p3 rib until sock measures 7in (18cm).

Ankle and foot

Move ribbing over by 1 st thus:
Next round: *p1, k3, p2, rep from * to end of round.
Rep last round twice.
Next round: *p2, k3, p1, rep from * to end of round.
Rep last round twice.
Cont as set, moving rib over by 1 st after each set of 3 rounds until sock measures 15in (38cm) or 1in (2.5cm) shorter than desired foot length.

Shape toe

Next round: K across.
Next round: *k1, k2tog, rep from * ending k1.
Rep last round until 8 sts rem.
Break off yarn leaving a good tail.

Making up

Place sts equally on 2 needles and graft together using Kitchener stitch.
Weave in any loose ends of yarn.

If your man needs some colourful persuasion to venture into the great outdoors, these may do the trick! They are guaranteed to keep out the cold.

Boot Sock

Size

To suit ankle circumference 8–13in (20–33cm)
Toe to heel 11½ in (29cm) adjustable

Tension

Not critical as fabric is stretchy.

Materials and Equipment

- Cygnet Wool-rich Machine-washable Chunky (148m per 100g)
- 1 x 100g ball in 2148 Petrole (A)
- 1 x 100g ball in 0268 Olive (B)
- 1 x 100g ball in 2185 Geranium (C)
- Set of 4mm (UK6:US8) double-pointed needles

Special techniques

- W1 = wrap 1
- Short row shaping
- Kitchener stitch

Method

Cast on 48 sts divided evenly between four needles.

Join, taking care not to twist sts.

Place marker at beg of round between N1 and N4.

Work in k2, p2 rib and in stripe pattern:

Stripe pattern

*8 rows A,

8 rows B,

1 row A, 8 rows C,

8 rows A,

5 rows B,

1 row A,

8 rows C,

7 rows B,

8 rows C,

8 rows A,

1 row C,

8 rows B,

rep from *as desired, working a single row of B between C and A on the foot.

Work striped rib for 18in (46cm) or desired length.

Shape heel

Use 20 sts, RS facing.

Row 1: K19, W1.

Row 2: P19 W1.

Rep last 2 rows working one stitch fewer (i.e. 18 sts on next 2 rows; 17 sts for following 2 rows) until 11 sts rem in work.

Next row: K11, pick up and k wrapped st, replace on LH needles, turn.

Next row: P11, pick up and p wrapped st, replace on LH needles, turn.

Next row: K12, pick up and k wrapped st, replace on LH needles, turn.

Next row: P12, pick up and p wrapped st, replace on LH needles, turn. Cont as set working one more st on each row until all 20 heel sts are back in work, then cont in rib patt across rest of sock (48 sts).

Work straight in st st (heel sts) and rib (upper sock) following stripe patt until sock 2in (5cm) shorter than required for toe.

Shape toe

Note: the toe is worked in a two-colour vertical stripe of 1 st A, 1 st B and the 2 st stripe sequence kept correct throughout.

Divide sts equally between four needles (12 sts per needle) and shape thus:

Decrease round

N1: K to last 3 sts, k2tog, k1.

N2: K1, skpo, k to end.

N3: K to last 3 sts, k2tog, k1.

N4: K1, skpo, k to end.

Cont as set, alternating dec and non-dec rounds, until 32 sts rem.

Work each round as a dec round until 8 sts rem.

Making up

Graft 8 sts tog using Kitchener stitch.

Weave in any loose ends of yarn.

The yarn used for this design was developed to produce socks with horizontal stripes – but this pattern is worked sideways, so the result is vertical stripes!

'On the Edge' Verticals

Size

To fit size small (medium: large) adult sizes

Tension

30 sts and 40 rows to 4in (10cm) in st st using
3.25mm needles
Use larger or smaller needles to achieve correct tension.

Materials and Equipment

- Kaffe Fassett for Regia 75% Wool and 25% Polyamide (210m per 50g)
- 3 × 50g balls 4256 Mirage Twilight.
- 2 × 3.25mm (UK10:US3) circular needles.

Special techniques

Kitchener stitch
Right-slanting dec: k2tog or p2tog
Left-slanting dec: skpo or ssp
M1R (see techniques)

Note: the socks are worked back and forth on a circular needle, which has the flexibility to accommodate the curve of the heel and toe. All even rows are RS rows, and all odd rows are WS rows. A second circular needle in the same size is used for grafting

Method

Note: markers are placed to divide the sections of the sock on row 1. The patterns used for each section are established on row 2.

Using a provisional cast-on method, cast on 113(117:118) sts.
Row 1: (WS) P38(38:37) foot sts, place foot marker; p13(14:15) heel sts, place centre heel marker; p13(14:15) heel sts, place leg marker; k41(43:43) leg sts, place cuff marker; p8 cuff sts.
Row 2: Work the cuff sts in dg-st (see below), starting with row 1 of patt; work the leg sts and heel sts in st st; work up to the last foot sts in st st, then work the edge st in the slip-stitch edge patt starting with row 1.

Double garter stitch (dg-st)

Row 1 (RS): Purl.
Row 2 (WS): Knit.
Row 3 (RS): Knit.
Row 4 (WS): Purl.

Slip-stitch edge

Row 1 (RS): Sl1 p-wise with yarn in front.
Row 2 (WS): K1 tbl.
Cont in patts as set, work 5 rows.

Heel shaping (1)

Row 8: Cont in patts as set, begin heel shaping by working paired dec on every row thus:
RS rows: Work to 2 sts before centre heel marker, k2tog, skpo, work to end.
WS rows: Work to 2 sts before centre heel marker, ssp, p2tog, work to end.
Rep this row 11(12:13) times.

Calf shaping

Row 19(20:21): Work as a dec row,. At the same time reposition the stitch markers, retaining the centre heel and cuff markers, removing the leg and the foot markers, and adding a centre toe marker 2 sts in from the end of the foot (inc edge st).
After this row, there should be 8 cuff sts, 41(43:43) edge sts, 2 heel sts and 38(38:37) foot sts or 89(91:90) sts.

Toe shaping

Row 20(21:22): Begin to work paired inc on every row thus:
RS rows: Work to 1 st before centre toe marker, M1R, k2, M1L, work to end.
WS rows: Work to 1 st before centre toe marker, M1L, p2, M1R, work to end.
Rep inc row 11(12:13) times until there are 13(15:16) sts between the centre toe marker and the end of the toe.
Row 31 (33:35): This completes the toe increases. After this row, there should be 8 cuff sts, 42(44:47) sts between the cuff and centre heel markers, 49(50:50) sts between the centre heel and centre toe markers and 14(15:16) sts from the centre toe marker to the end of the row, a total of 113(117:118)sts.
Work 8 rows.

Complete toe

Row 48(50:52): Begin working paired dec on every row thus:
RS rows: Work to 2 sts before centre toe marker, k2tog, skpo, work to end.
WS rows: Work to 2 sts before centre toe marker, ssp, p2tog, work to end. Rep dec row 11(12:13) times so there are 8 cuff sts, 41(43:43) leg sts, 2 heel sts (1 st either side of centre heel marker) and 38(38:37) foot sts, 89(91:90) sts in total.

Heel shaping (2)

Row 60(63:66): Begin working paired inc for second half of heel shaping on every row thus:

RS rows: Work to 1 st before centre heel marker, M1R, k2, M1L, work to end.

WS rows: Work to 1 st before centre heel marker, M1L, p2, M1R, work to end. Rep inc row 11(12:13) times and at the same time:

Row 68(72:76): Cont to work the leg sts in g st.

Row 71(75:79): This should be the last row of heel increases. After this, there should be 8 cuff sts, 54(57:58) sts between the cuff and centre heel markers, 51(52:52) sts between the centre heel marker and end of row, 113(117:118) sts.

Work straight for a further 8 rows ending with row 79(83:91).

Making up

Remove the provisional cast on and place the resulting 'live' loops on the second circular needle.

Cut the working yarn leaving a long tail, and thread this on a tapestry needle. Fold work in half, RS together, bring needles parallel to one another and, working from right to left, graft the two sides together.

Working along the sides of the foot and toe, pick up the sts between the edge sts so you have 20(21:22) sts on the needle. Graft these sts together in the same way as the main sock seam.

Turn finished sock inside out to produce the effect.

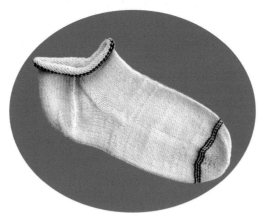

These gym socks are made from a hard-wearing stretch yarn that ensures a perfect ft. Choose shades to complement your sportsman's kit.

Stretchy Gym Socks

Size

To fit men's size medium (large)

Tension

Not critical as yarn is stretchy and length may be adjusted.

Materials and Equipment

- Elle stretch DK (155m per 50g ball)
- 1 x 50g ball in white (M).
- Cygnet 4 ply
- Oddment in navy (C)
- Set of 2.75mm (UK12:US2) double-pointed needles

Special techniques

- Garter stitch in rounds = 1 row knit, 1 row purl
- Stocking stitch (st st) in rounds = knit each round
- Three-needle cast-off (see techniques section)

Method

Cast on 52(56) sts loosely.

Divide the sts so there are 18(20) sts on N1; 20(22) sts on N2 and 18(20) sts on N3.

Using C, work 12 rounds garter stitch.

Using M work 8 rounds stocking stitch.

Heel flaps

Arrange 13(14) sts on N1; 26(28) sts on N2 and 13(14) sts on N3.

Next row: Work straight on the sts on N2 only for 26(28) rows.

Turn heel

Row 1: K5, skpo, k to last 7 sts k2tog, k5.

Row 2 and every alt row: Purl.

Rep last 2 rows until 16 sts rem.

Instep

Pick up 16(17) sts along edge of heel flap, picking up from knit rows only for a clean finish; k sts on N1 and N2; pick up 15 (16) sts on opposite edge of heel flap; k to end (74 sts).

Rearrange sts so there are 24(25) sts on N1; 26 sts on N2 and 24 (25) sts on N3.

Instep decrease

Round 1: K to last 3 sts on N1, k2tog k1; k all sts on N2; k to last 3 sts on N3, skpo.

Rep last round 11 times.

Rearrange sts so there are 14 sts on N1; 26(28) sts on N2 and 13(14) sts on N3.

Tip

A smooth finish is essential for this sock to prevent any danger of rubbing. When picking up stitches along the edge of the heel flap, pick up only from the end of knit rows.

Foot

Work 50 rounds.

Shape toe

Round 1: Using C, p.

Round 2: Using M, p to last 3 sts on N1, p2tog, p1; on N2 p1, p2tog, p to last 3 sts, p2tog p1; on N3 p1, p2tog, p to end.

Round 3: K.

Rep last 2 rounds until 20 (24) sts rem.

Cast off using three-needle cast off.

Making up

Sew in ends.

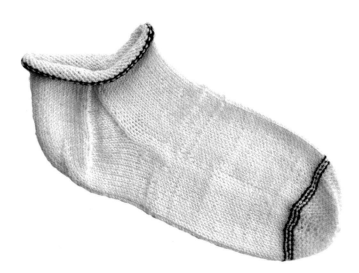

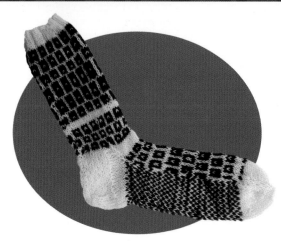

These should be snazzy enough to make your man go that extra mile in his walking boots. They have an interesting squared heel, and the pattern is based on old tiles.

Whizzy Walkers

Size
Ankle circumference 8in (20cm)
Toe to heel 9in (22.5cm)

Tension
24 sts and 28 rounds to 4in (10cm) measured over patt.
Use larger or smaller needles to achieve correct tension.

Materials and Equipment
- 4-ply sock wool (approx 198 yards per 50g ball)
- 2 x 50g balls brown (M)
- 2 x 50g balls cream (C)
- Set of 4mm (UK8:US6) double-pointed needles

Special techniques
- Double decrease: slip 2 sts, k1, pass both sl sts over k st.

Note: the examples have been worked using the same yarn but with the main and contrast reversed for the second sock.

Leg

Using M, cast on 50 sts and divide evenly between 3 needles. Join into a round being careful not to twist sts.

Note: this join marks a seam and the beginning of a round, so place a marker here if desired.

Work 6 rows k1, p1 rib.

Next round: Inc 1 st at each end of round (52 sts).

Beg working pattern from chart to marked row, but dec 1 st at each end on last round (50 sts).

Divide sts so there are 12 sts on N1, 25 sts on N2 and 13 sts on N3 (seam line between N1 and N3).

Using N3, k across 11 sts on N1; yf, sl1. Set aside the 25 sts on N2 for instep and work the heel on 25 sts.

Turn work.

Shape heel

Row 1: K1 tbl, p23, yf, sl1, turn.
Row 2: K1 tbl, *k1, sl1 p-wise, rep from * to end, turn.
Row 3: K16, k2tog tbl, turn.
Row 4: *Sl1, p7, p2tog, turn.
Row 5: Sl1 (K1, sl1) three times, k1, k2tog tbl, turn.

Rep last 2 rows until all sts either side of the 9 central heel sts have been worked off.

Gusset

Next row: Using N1 (Sl1, k1) 4 times, k1, pick up 13 sts tbl along R heel flaps; using N2, pick up and k1 st tbl at beg of instep sts, k across 25 instep sts; pick up and k1 st at end of instep; using N3, k13 tbl from L of heel flap, slip the first 4 sts from heel flap on to N3. There should now be 18 sts on N1, 27 sts on N2 and 17 sts on N3.

Next round: K to last 2 sts on N1, k2tog; work k2tog tbl at the beg of N2, k to last 2 sts, k2 tog; at the beg of N3 k2tog tbl, k to end.

Next round: Follow patt on top of foot and *at the same time* dec 1 st at the end of N1 and the beg of N3 as before. Repeat until there are 13 sts on N1, 25 sts on N2 and 12 sts on N3

Work straight, working chart B twice on top of foot and sole in M until foot measures 2.5cm less than length required. Cont in M only.

Shape toe

Round 1: K to last 2 sts on N1, sl2 k-wise; k1 from N2 and pass slipped sts from N1 over this k1, work to last 2 sts on N2, sl2 k-wise; k1 from N3 and pass slipped sts from N2 over this K1.

Round 2: K.

Rep last 2 rows until 6 sts rem on N1, 13 sts on N2, 6 sts on N3.

Now work double dec every round until 6 sts in total rem.

Making up

Draw thread through rem sts and draw up. Weave loose end firmly back into work and stitch to finish.

Ankle and top of foot chart

12 sts x 38 rows

 M C

start of heel

toe

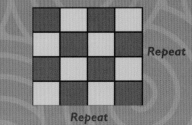

Sole pattern

Repeat

Repeat

These wonderfully warm toddler socks are really fast to make.
The easy heel eliminates the need to pick up stitches.

Easy Heel Toddler

Size

To suit ankle circumference 6½in (17cm)

Tension

20 sts and 30 rows to 4in (10cm) over stocking stitch
using 3mm needles
Use larger or smaller needles to achieve correct tension.

Materials and Equipment

- Debbie Bliss Rialto extra-fine merino (105m per 50g ball).
- 1 x 50g ball in 01 White (M)
- 1 x 50g ball in 13 Pink (C)
- Set of 3mm (UK11:US2–3) double-pointed needles

Special techniques

- Easy (no turn) heel
- Kitchener stitch
- M1 by picking up 1 st in gap between needles
  and working in the back
- Skpo (slip 1, k1, pass slipped stitch over to decrease)

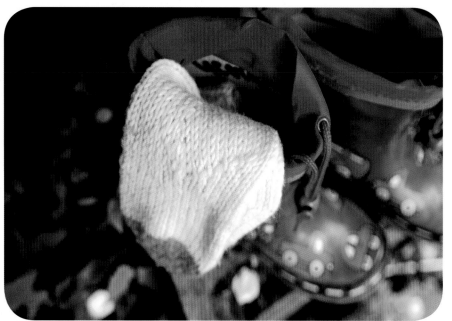

Heel decreases

Round 1: K9 on N1; k1, k2tog, k11 on N2; k11, k2tog, k1 on N3 (35 sts).
Round 2: K9 on N1; k1, k2tog, k10 on N2; k10, k2tog, k1 on N3 (33 sts).
Round 3: K9 on N1; k1, k2tog, k9 on N2; k9, k2tog, k1 on N3 (31 sts).
Round 4: K9 on N1; k1, k2tog, k8 on N2; k8, k2tog, k1 on N3 (29 sts).
Round 5: K9 on N1; k1, k2tog, k7 on N2; k7, k2tog, k1 on N3 (27 sts).
Work 15 rows st st.
Divide sts between three needles so there are 7 sts on N1 for the left side, 13 sts on N2 for the top foot and 7 sts on N3 for the right side.
Change to C to begin toe decreases.

Method

Using M, cast on 27 sts divided evenly between 4 needles.
Join, taking care not to twist sts.
Work in k, p1 rib for 8 rows.
Knit 15 rows.
Stitches will be increased over the next 11 rounds.
Rearrange sts over 3 needles so there are 7 sts on N1, 13 sts on N2 and 7 sts on N3, and mark the beg of the round with a stitch marker.

Heel shaping

Round 1: K7 sts from N1, m1, k13 sts from N2, m1, k7 sts from N3 (29 sts)
Round 2 and every alternate round: Knit all sts.
Round 3: K7 on N1, m1, k14 on N2, m1, k8 on N3 (31 sts).
Round 5: K7 on N1, m1, k15 on N2, m1, k9 on N3 (33 sts).
Round 7: K7 on N1, m1, k16 on N2, m1, k10 on N3 (35 sts) .
Round 9: K7 on N1, m1, k17 on N2, m1, k11 on N3 (37 sts).
Round 10: Knit all sts.
Rearrange sts so there are 9 sts on N1, 14 sts on N2 and 14 sts on N3 (37 sts).
Stitches will now be decreased to give the angle required for the heel shape.

Toe

Round 1: K to last 3 sts on N1, k2 tog, k1; k1, skpo, k to end of N2; k to last 3 sts on N3, k2tog, k1.
Round 2: Knit all sts.
Rep these two rounds until 4 sts rem.

Making up

Using Kitchener stitch, graft toe stitches together.
Press lightly.

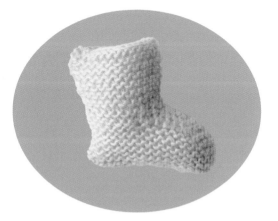

Treat a baby you know with these simple but special garter stitch socks in two sizes. The first size fits the tiniest newborn while the second size is suitable for a baby up to about nine months.

The Very First Pair

Size

- For newborn size follow first set of instructions
- For approx 3-9 months follow second set of instructions

Tension

Not critical as the garter stitch fabric is stretchy

Measurements

- Cygnet 4-ply (205m per 50g ball) or oddment of any 4-ply yarn
- 1 × 50g ball
- A pair of 3mm (UK11:US2-3) needles en dash

Special techniques

- Sl1 wyf = take yarn forward, slip 1 st with yarn forward, take yarn back to work next st
- Sl1 wyb = slip 1 st with yarn at the back of work

First size
(make two the same)
Cast on 34 sts.

Work 14 rows g-st (every row knit).

Next row: K20, k2tog, turn (half the sts plus the sts for centre panel)

Next row: Sl1 wyf, k6, k2tog.

Next row: Sl1 wyb k6, k2tog.

Rep the last 2 rows, working back and forth on centre sts and picking up 1 st from the sides in the k2 tog at either end, until there are 24 sts in total on the needles; k to end.

Cuff
Work 20 rows on these 24 sts to make roll-over cuff.

Cast off and join centre back seam.

Second size
(make two the same)
Cast on 54 sts.

Work 14 rows g-st.

Next row: K31, k2tog, turn.

Next row: Sl1 wyf, k8, k2tog.

Next row: S1 wyb, k8, k2tog.

Rep the last 2 rows, working ba forth on centre sts and picking from the sides in the k2 tog at end, until there are 35 sts in tot the needles; k to end.

Cuff
Work 20 rows on these 35 sts to make roll-over cuff.

Cast off and join centre back seam.

Tip
One ball of yarn should be enough to make three socks. Why not make a spare in case baby loses one?

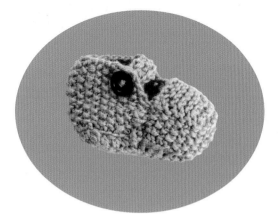

This must be the cutest little shoe sock ever – and it's really easy
to make on two needles.

Moss Stitch Shoesocks

Size
To fit age 6–9 months

Tension
12 sts and 16 rows to 4in (10cm) over stocking
stitch using 3.75mm needles

Materials and Equipment
- Sirdar Sublime Cashmerino silk DK (116m per 50g).
- 1 x 50g ball in 0006
- Pair of 3.75mm (UK9:US5) needles.
- 2 buttons

Special techniques
- Moss stitch

Note: a short 3.75mm (UK9:US5) circular needle may be substituted to work the sock top and sides.

Method

Cast on 32 sts and work 2 rows moss st.
Buttonhole row: Moss st 2, yf, k2tog, moss st to end.
Next row: Cast off 11 sts, moss st to end (21 sts).
Work 5 rows moss st.
Cut yarn and leave sts on stitch holder.

Sock top

Cast on 7 sts and work 13 rows g-st.
Cut working yarn.
With RS facing rejoin yarn at R side of sock top.
Pick up and k7 sts up R side, k7 sts across top, pick up and k7 sts down L side; moss stitch across 21 sts on stitch holder, ensuring buttonhole is to L of needle (49 sts).
Work 7 rows moss stitch.
Next row: Cast off 7 sts, moss st 7 sts, cast off 28 sts.
Rejoin yarn to rem 7 sts and work 23 rows.
Cast off.

Making up

Join side and foot seams.
Sew on buttons to correspond with buttonholes.

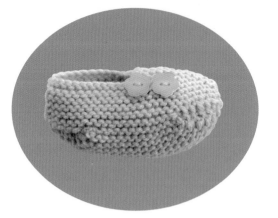

These simple garter stitch slippers in softest cashmere yarn
are worked in garter stitch. There are three sizes to fit your little one
from birth to three years of age.

Baby Pods

Size

To To fit 0–6(6–9:18–36) months.

Tension

Not critical

Materials and Equipment

- Cashmere or cashmere-mix DK yarn
- 1 x 50g ball in pale pink
- A pair of 3mm (UK11: US2–3) needles
- 2 buttons (optional)

Special techniques

- Kitchener stitch

Next row: Cast on 7 sts for the heel 19(23:27) sts.

Work straight, inc 1 st at toe edge every alt row until there are 25(29:33) sts.

Next row: Cast off 12(15:18) sts at heel, k to end.

Work 13(15:17) rows, casting on 12(15:18) sts at heel end of last row 25(29:33) sts.

Keeping the heel edge straight, dec 1 st at toe edge on every alt row until 19(23:27) sts rem.

Cast off.

Making up

Join seam up back of heel.

Attach sole to top, easing stitches in as necessary.

Attach buttons if desired, taking care to produce a 'left' and 'right' bootee!

Tip

The shape of these little boots when you are working them is very odd, so do not worry. All will become clear when you join the seams!

Top

Cast on 15(19:22) sts.

Next row: Inc in first st, k to last st, inc in last st.

Rep this row until there are 22(30:38) sts.

Shape heel

Next row: Cast on 7(8:8) sts, work to end.

Work straight, inc 1 st at end of each row until there are 29(37:43) sts.

Work 2 rows without shaping.

Work straight, dec 1 st at each end of next and every foll alt row until 12(16:20) sts rem.

Treat a baby you know with these cute socks. The example was worked in luxurious hand-dyed, hand-spun silk, but any 2-ply yarn can be used.

Cutie Babe Socks

Size
0–9 (9–18) months

Materials and Equipment
- 2-ply yarn
- 1 x 50g ball
- A pair of 2.75–3mm (UK11–12:US2) bamboo needles

Sole

Cast on 34 (54) sts.
Work 14 rows k.

Top foot

Next row: K20 (31) sts, k2tog, turn,
leaving rem sts on holder.
Next row: Yf, sl1, p6(8), p2tog, turn.
Next row: Sl1, k6(8), k2tog.
Working back and forth on centre sts,
rep last 2 rows 7 times.

Ankle cuff

Next 2 rows: K to end, including sts
from holder (24:35) sts
Work 20 rows.
Cast off.

Making up

Join centre back seam

This adorable sock is ideal for baby's first official engagement.
The sprinkling of glass beads adds an extra-special touch.

Cashmere Celebration

Size
To suit age 0–9 months

Tension
Not critical

Materials and Equipment
- Filatura di Crosa Superior (330 yds/300m per 25g ball)
- Set of 2mm (UK14:US0) double-pointed needles
- 2 small buttons
- Approx 16 silver–lined glass beads

Special techniques
- Garter stitch in the round (k1 round, p1 round)

Strap

K17, cast on 11 sts for strap.

Work 2 rows on these 28 sts.

Next row (buttonhole): Work to last 3 sts, k2tog, yo, k1.

Knit 1 row.

Cast off.

Making up

Join the sole seam. Sew button to strap. Attach beads to front of shoe as shown.

Sole

Cast on 31 sts and divide evenly between needles. Join into a round, taking care not to twist sts.

Work in g-st.

Round 1: K.

Round 2: Inc in first st, p13, inc, p1, inc, p to last st, inc (35 sts).

Rounds 3, 5 and 7: K.

Round 4: Inc in first st, p14, inc, p3, inc, p1, inc, p to last st, inc (39 sts).

Round 6: Inc in first st, p15, inc, p5, inc, p to last st, inc (43 sts).

Round 8: Inc in first st, p16, inc, p7, inc, p to last st, inc (47 sts).

Side and top

Change to st st (every round knit) and work 9 rounds.

Next round: K13, (skpo) 5 times, k1 (k2tog) 5 times, k13 (37 sts).

Next round: K9, cast off 19, k8, turn. Work 1 row using 2 needles on these 17 sts.

These cotton shoe socks are full of fun for tiny toes. The examples were worked In zingy lemon and lime to stimulate the senses.

Fizzy Feet

Size

To fit age 6–9 months

Tension

23 sts and 29 rows to 4in (10cm) over stocking stitch

Materials and Equipment

- Rowan Cotton Glace 100% cotton (137yds/115m per 50g ball)
- 1 x 50g ball in 833 Ochre (M)
- 1 x 50g ball in 814 Shoot (C)
- A pair of size 3mm (UK11:US2–3) needles
- 2 buttons

Sole

Using C, cast on 38 sts and work 10 rows g-st.
Change to M and work 8 rows g-st.
Next row: K17, (k2tog) twice, K17 (36 sts).
Work 3 rows g-st.

Shape top

Next row: K8, cast off 7 sts, k6, cast off 7 sts, k8.
Slip 8 sts from each end of row on to a safety pin.
Rejoin yarn to centre 6 sts and work 6 rows g-st for a T-bar.

Ankle strap

Next row: Cast on 7 sts, turn.
Next row: K7, k6 from front strap, cast on 7 sts, k8 from stitch holder, cast on 9 sts for strap wrapover (37 sts).
Next row: K, including sts from rem stitch holder (46 sts)
Work 4 rows g-st.
Buttonhole row: K2, yf, k2tog, k to end.
Work 1 row k.
Change to C and work 1 row k.
Cast off.

Second shoe

Work as for first shoe to buttonhole row, then work thus:

Buttonhole row: K to last 4 sts, k2tog, yf, k2.
Work 1 row k.
Change to C and work 1 row k.
Cast off.

Making up

Join sole and back of heel.
Attach button to correspond with buttonhole.

These must be the most adorable little shoe socks ever, and they are really easy and quick to make. Use up any oddments of 3-ply yarn for this design.

Mary Janes

Size

To fit age 6–9 months

Tension

Use smallest needles for smallest size

Materials and Equipment

- 50g any 3 ply yarn (examples were made using Cygnet 3-ply and Colinette silk).
- A pair of 3mm (UK11:US2–3), or 3.5mm (UK9–10:US4) or 4mm (UK8:US6) needles
- 2 buttons

Method

Cast on 31 sts and work in g-st throughout.

Row 1: K.

Row 2: Inc in first st, k13, inc 1, k1, inc 1, k to last st, inc in last st (35 sts).

Row 3: K.

Row 4: Inc in first st, k14, inc 1, k3, inc 1, k1, inc 1, k to last st, inc in last st (39 sts).

Row 5: K.

Row 6: Inc in first st, k15, inc 1, k5, inc 1, k1, inc 1, k to last st, inc in last st (43 sts).

Row 7: K.

Row 8: Inc in first st, k16, inc 1, k7, inc 1, k1, inc 1, k to last st, inc in last st (47 sts).

Change to st st and work 9 rows.

Next row: K13, (skpo) 5 times, k1, (k2tog) 5 times, k13 (37 sts).

Shape strap

Next row: K9, cast off 19, k8.

Next row: K.

Next row: K17, cast on 11 sts for strap.

Buttonhole row: K to last 3 sts, k2 tog, yo k1.

Work 1 row

Cast off.

Making up

Press lightly.

Join seam (sole and back). Sew on button to correspond with buttonhole.

Flower

Cast on 33 sts and k 3 rows.

Row 4: K3, twist all of work on needle 360 degrees, *k3 twist again, rep from * to end.

Row 5: *K2tog, rep from * to last st, k1 (17 sts).

Row 6: *K2tog, rep from * to end.

Thread yarn through rem sts and curl into rosette shape.

Attach securely to top of shoe.

A naked foot!

Techniques

How to make your feet even more beautiful

Successful socks

Knitting socks is fun and surprisingly easy, but taking the time to read through these guidelines before you begin will greatly increase your chance of success. Socks are usually worked not in rows but in rounds, on circular or double-pointed needles. The advantage of this is that there are no seams to sew up, or to rub!

The foot section of a good basic sock should be roughly one-third the length of the finished sock. Check the actual measurements of the foot and leg before you begin and adjust the pattern if necessary. Experiment with different heel and toe styles, then incorporate your favourites in any design you make.

How to knit a sock

Cast on firmly but cast off fairly loosely. For extra elasticity, cast on twice as many stitches as required for the top of the sock, then work two stitches together all the way along the first row to return to the correct number. Work as evenly as possible to prevent your socks losing their shape in the wash.

For a knee-high sock, work the ribbing, then work approximately as many rounds are there stitches on the needles before starting to decrease. Work decreases on either side of the central 'seam' stitch, until at the ankle the number of stitches is approximately three-quarters of the number cast on.

For the **ankle** section, work approximately as many rounds are there are stitches on the needle before starting to decrease. Then, keeping the 'seam' stitch central, place half the stitches on a needle for the heel. Divide the remaining stitches equally between two needles for the instep, and set aside until the heel has been worked.

The length of the finished **heel,** laid flat, should be the same as the width of the ankle. Pick up as many stitches along the heel flap and are on the needle st the top of the heel and the

instep – roughly 8-10 fewer stitches than the number of stitches cast on. If there are fewer loops than stitches that need to be picked up, increase evenly as necessary.

For the **gusset,** decrease on alternate rounds until there are the same number of stitches as on the ankle. The **toe** of an average-sized adult sock should be about 2½ in (5cm) long.

Tip

Work a swatch of yarn until you are happy with the effect Measure carefully to calculate the number of stitches you need. Deduct approximately 10 per cent to allow for the sock to stretch and ensure a snug fit. Make sure the resulting number is divisible by four.

Tension

When you begin to knit socks, start a habit that will save a lot of time in the end: work a swatch using the chosen yarn and needles. These can be labelled and filed for future reference. Many sock yarns are a 4-ply weight. When knitting socks in 4-ply, a tension of 68 sts to 4in (10cm) width on size 2.25mm (UK13–14/US0–1) needles or 48 sts on size 3.5mm (UK9–10/US4) works well.

Needles

Most of the socks in this book are worked on double-pointed needles. For sections of the sock that are not worked in the round, such as heels and gussets, just use the same needles and work back and forth. Socks may also be worked using circular needles if preferred. A few designs are worked on straight needles, so there are seams to join. 'On the Edge' designs are worked back and forth on circular needles.

Yarn

Socks may be made in a huge variety of yarns, from luxurious cashmere to smooth, cool cotton. There are also many yarns on the market that are specifically designed for socks. A good choice for socks is a yarn made mainly from wool for warmth, with a little added nylon for strength.

Substituting yarn

It is relatively simple to substitute different yarns for any of the socks in this book, but remember to check your tension. One way to substitute yarn is to work out how many wraps per inch (wpi) the yarn produces. Do this by winding it closely, in a single layer, round a rule or similar object and counting how many 'wraps' to an inch (5cm) it produces. For a successful result, pick a yarn that produces twice, or a little more than twice, the number of wraps per inch (or slightly more) as there are stitches per inch in the tension swatch.

Tension required	Use yarn with this no of WPI
8 sts per in (4-ply/fingering)	16 - 18 wpi
6.5 sts per in (DK/sport)	13 - 14 wpi
5.5 sts per in (Chunky/worsted)	11 – 12wpi

Casting on

There are several well-known ways to cast on. Everyone has a favourite, but it is essential that the cast-on should be elastic. Here are three:

Basic cast on

This method produces a purl stitch as a base.

1 Make a slip knot and place on the left-hand hand needle. Insert the right-hand needle into the loop and wrap the yarn round the needles as shown.

2 Using the point of the right-hand needle, pull the yarn through the first loop to create a second loop.

3 Slide it onto the left-hand needle.
Slide the loop on to the left-hand needle so there are two loops on the needle.

Repeat step 2 and step 3 until you have the desired number of stitches on your needle.

Continental or long tail cast on

This makes a firm, smoothly twisted elastic edge and only one needle is used.

- Make a slip knot and place on the tip of the hand needle. Leave a tail about three times as long as the edge you want to cast on. Take the tail behind your left thumb and the working yarn round your forefinger, and secure the long ends using your remaining fingers. Twist your wrist so your palm is upwards, then spread your thumb and index finger so the yarn forms a V-shape.

- Slide the needle through the loop on your thumb and catch the working yarn round your right forefinger from right to left. Draw the new stitch though, letting the loop slip off your thumb and over the tip of the needle. Catch the tail of the yarn again and pull gently to tighten the new stitch.

- Repeat until required number of stitches are on needle.

1

2

3

Provisional cast on

Using this method you will be able to work in either direction from the starting point

- Make a loop near the end of the working yarn and pull up tight on needle. Take some waste yarn the length of the cast-on you need plus 15in (40cm) and make a loop near the end. With the needle in your right hand and facing left, slide the loop of waste yarn on to the needle, next to the loop of working yarn. Hold the tails of both lengths of yarn to keep them out of the way.

- Insert index finger from behind between working and waste yarns. Twist finger 90° clockwise. Slide thumb next to index finger between waste/working yarns and spread yarns apart: index finger should hold waste and thumb working yarn. Hold the tails of both yarns with the rest of the fingers on your right hand to keep them taut. Twist yarns 90° clockwise and wrap waste yarn round needle.

- ***** twist yarns 180° clockwise and wrap waste yarn round needle. Twist yarns anti-clockwise 180° and wrap waste yarn round needle*****. Repeat from * to * until there are the desired number of stitches on the needle.

Note: when you begin knitting make sure waste yarn is under the first stitch to hold the loop. Leave in place until you need to use the stitches it is holding.

Casting off

- Knit two stitches using the right-hand needle, then slip the first stitch over the second and let it drop over the needle as shown.

- Knit another stitch so there are two stitches on the right-hand needle. Repeat the process. When only one stitch remains, break yarn and thread through the stitch.

Three-needle cast off

Divide sts equally between two needles and place needles parallel to each other.
Step 1: *using a third needle, pick up 1 st from N1 and 1 st from N2 and k sts tog. Repeat, so that there are 2 sts on N3.
Step 2: Pass RH st on N3 over LH st on N3 to cast off. Repeat from * to end.

Tip
Whichever method you choose, it is vital to check the elasticity of the cast-on. Remember that the sock needs enough stretch to go over the foot then be pulled up and stay up! If you tend to cast on tightly use a needle one size larger for the cast on.

Measurements

For a standard sock, the width of the leg is the same as the width of the foot. For a good fit, measure the widest part of your leg and the widest part of your foot. One way to achieve a perfect fit is to work the sock from the toe up, which also eliminates the need to graft stitches on the toe. Another method is to work socks as a tube leaving aside the heel area, which is worked last. This method is ideal when following a complicated charted design

This chart is a guide to sock sizing based on shoe sizes. The babies' foot size chart that follows is based on average sizes. Measure very carefully as charts and shoe sizes may vary.

Tip

Quick converter – use our quick guide to find your size

Adult female

8 –10½in (20–26.5cm)

Adult male

10½–12in (27–30.5cm)

Size chart
for babies & children

Size/age of baby	Foot length
3–5lbs	2½in–3in (7.5cm)
5–7lbs	3–3½in (7.5–9cm)
7–9lbs *(most common size for newborns)*	3½–3¾in (8.25–9.5cm)
3–6 months	4–4½in (10–11.5cm)
6 months–1 year	4¼–4¾in (10.5–12cm)
18 months–2 years	5–5 ½in (12.5–14cm)
2–3 years	5–6in (13.25–15cm)
8 years	7in (17.75cm)
12 years	8–8½in (20–21.5cm)

European shoe size	UK shoe size	US shoe size	Width round top of cuff	Heel flap length	Total foot length
Infants/toddlers					
18–20		3–5	5⅓in (13.5cm)	1in (2.5cm)	5⅛in (13cm)
22–23		6–7½	5⅞in (15cm)	1⅛in (2.75cm)	5⅞in (15cm)
24–25		8–8½	6⅛in (15.5cm)	1⅓in (3.5cm)	6in (16cm)
Children					
26–27		9–10	6⅜in (16cm)	1½in (4cm)	7⅛in (18cm)
28–29		10½–11½	6⅔in (16.75cm)	1½in (4cm)	7in (19cm)
30–31		12–12½	6⅞in (17.5cm)	1¾in (4.5cm)	8⅛in (20.5cm)
Children/adult women					
32–33		13–1	7¼in (18.5cm)	1¾in (4.5cm)	8⅔in (22cm)
34–35		2–3	7½in (19cm)	1⅞in (4.75cm)	9⅛in (23cm)
36–37		4–5	7¾in (19.5cm)	1⅞in (4.75cm)	9⅝in (24.5cm)
38–39		6–7	8in (20.25cm)	2⅛in (5.25cm)	10¼in (26cm)
40–41		8–9	8¼in (20.5cm)	2¼in (5.5cm)	10⅝in (27cm)
42-43		10–11	8½in (21.5cm)	2¼in (5.75in)	11in (28cm)
Adult men					
42-43		8–9	8½in (21.5cm)	2¼in (2.75cm)	11in (28cm)
44–45		10–10½	9in (22.75cm)	2½in (6.5cm)	11½in (29cm)
46-47		11–12	9⅛in (23cm)	2½in (6.5cm)	12in (30.5cm)

Knit stitch

1 Hold the needle with the cast-on stitches in your left hand. Place the tip of the empty right-hand needle into the first stitch. Wrap the yarn around as for casting on.

2 Pull the yarn through the needle to create a new loop.

3 Slip the new stitch on to the right-hand needle.

Continue in the same way for each stitch on the left-hand needle.

To start a new row, exchange the needles so that the left needle is full once again and repeat instructions.

Purl stitch

1. Hold the yarn to the front of the work as shown.

2. Place the right needle into the first stitch from front to back. Wrap the yarn around right needle in an anti-clockwise direction as shown.

3. Bring the needle down and back through the stitch, and pull through.

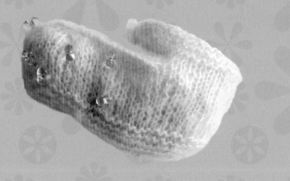

Types of stitches

1 Garter stitch

Knit every row.
In the round, knit 1 row, purl 1 row.

2 Stocking stitch

Knit RS rows; purl WS rows.
In the round, knit every row.

3 Single rib

With an even number of stitches:
Row 1: *k1, p1* rep to end.
Rep for each row.
With an odd number of stitches:
Row 1: *k1, p1, rep from * to last stitch, k1.
Row 2: *p1, k1, rep from * to last stitch, p1.

4 Double rib

Row 1: *k2, p2, rep from * to end.
Rep for each row.

5 Moss stitch

Starting with an even number of stitches:
Row 1: (K1, P1) to end.
Row 2: (P1, K1) to end.
Rep rows 1 and 2 to form pattern.
Starting with an odd number of stitches:
Row 1: *K1, P1, rep from * to last st, K1.
Rep to form pattern.

6 Cable stitch

These decorative stitches are easy to work using a cable needle. Stitches are held on the cable needle, then worked later to create twists. The example shows 2 sts being cabled, but the method is the same for any number of stitches.

Cable 2F

A Slip the next 2 sts on to a cable needle and hold in front of work.

B Knit the next 2 sts from the left needle, then k2 from the cable needle.

Cable 2B

C Slip 2 sts on to a cable needle and hold at back of work; k2 from left needle, then k2 from cable needle.

Techniques

Working in the round

Many knitters are scared to try working in the round, but it is quite easy once you have mastered the basics. It is also the fastest way to knit: there are no seams to join, and the right side of the work is always facing, so working patterns is easier. Here are three ways of knitting in the round:

Tip

To avoid the dreaded dpn 'ladder' effect, rearrange the stitches on the needles every few rounds to move the stress points. One way to do this is by working two extra stitches from the next needle. Take care to mark the beginning of the actual round, or you will find it hard to tell where it technically begins.

Working with double-pointed needles

These usually come in sets of four or five. Reserve one needle to work with and space the cast-on stitches evenly between the remaining needles

1 Cast on the required number of stitches, divided equally between three needles. Lay the work flat to check that it is not twisted.

2 Insert a fourth needle (the 'working' needle) into the first stitch on needle 3 (N3), and knit the stitch. The yarn will be coming from the last stitch on N1, so working the first stitch will join the work. Pull the first few stitches tighter than in normal knitting to keep the join snug and avoid gaps between stitches. Then simply work the stitches from each needle as you come to it, round and round.

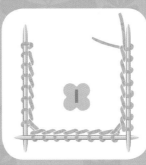

Working with circular needles

First, choose the correct needle. Its length should be roughly equal to, or less than, the circumference of what you are making. A 16in (40cm) circular needle is ideal for small items including baby garments and hats. For larger garments, use a 24in (60cm) needle and for a man's sweater use a 29in (75cm) or 32in (80cm) needle. For socks, use the smallest needle available.

Cast on across the right-hand needle so the first stitch is at the tip of the left-hand needle. Before joining the work, place a marker on the right-hand needle. Make sure the ridges at the bottom of the cast-on edge are facing the same way and are not twisted round the needle.

Insert the right-hand needle into the first stitch on the left needle and knit it. Continue to work the stitches from the left-hand to the right-hand needle, pulling the first few stitches firmly to keep the join snug, until you reach the marker. Slip the marker across and continue working round and round, from left to right without turning. The right side of the work will always be facing.

In circular knitting, work stocking stitch by knitting every row. For garter stitch, work one round knit, one round purl.

Magic loop

Magic loop knitting is a technique that allows you to use a circular needle of any size. As you work, simply pull the excess loop of cable through at the end of every round. You may prefer this, but try my method first.

Working with two circular needles

This idea of working two socks simultaneously on separate circular needles has become increasingly popular. It is appealing because both socks are completed at the same time. To prevent 'ladders', maintain a steady tension, especially near the circular joins.

Choose circular needles 16-24in (40-60cm) long, as appropriate. It is helpful if the needles look different. After casting on, heel stitches remain on needle 1 and instep stitches remain on needle 2.

When stitches are at rest, move them to the flexible section of the needle to provide the necessary 'give'.

- Using the first circular needle, cast on the required number of stitches.

- Slip the instep stitches to a second circular needle.

- Still using the first circular needle, cast on the number of stitches required for the second sock. Take care to cast on to the end of the needle, away from the first sock's yarn supply.

- Slip the instep stitches for the second sock to the second needle. The yarn supply for both socks should now be in the same position.

Sock decreases

Sock increases

Methods of decreasing are interchangeable, so choose the one you prefer, but remember to use it consistently for a neat overall appearance. Use a left-slanting decrease at the beginning of a needle and the right-slanting decrease at the end of a needle.

Left-slanting decreases
Ssk
Slip 2 sts knitwise, return sts to left needle, place the needle into the back of the yarn loops, and knit them together.

ssk (variation)
Slip 1st knitwise, then 1 st purlwise, return the sts to the left needle, then knit them together through the back of loops.

Ssp
Slip 2 sts knitwise, return the sts to the left needle, then purl them together through the back of the loops.

Skpo
Slip 1 st knitwise, k1, then pass the slipped stitch over the knitted st.

K2tog tbl
Knit two stitches together through the back of the yarn loops

Right-slanting decrease
K2tog
Knit two stitches together through the front of the loops.

There are many different ways to increase stitches, and knitters tend to stick with what they prefer. As with decreases, use the same method of increasing throughout a garment to ensure the best effect.

Simple increase
The easiest way to increase is by working twice into a stitch. To do this knitwise, simply knit the stitch as normal but do not remove the loop from the left-hand needle. Wrap the yarn over the needle again and knit into the back of the stitch before removing the loop from the left-hand needle.

M1R = make one stitch slanting to the right
Find the horizontal connecting yarn between the needles. Using the left needle, pick up the connecting yarn **from the back to the front** and leave this 'raised bar' on the left needle. Work the raised bar by knitting (RS row) or purling (WS row) as appropriate.

M1L = make one stitch slanting to the left
Find the horizontal connecting yarn between the needles. Using the left needle, pick up the connecting yarn **from the front to the back** and leave this 'raised bar' on the left needle. Then either knit the raised bar through the back of the loop (RS row) or purl the raised bar (WS row).

Joining seams

Stocking stitch joins

The edges of stocking stitch tend to curl so it may be tricky to join. The best way to join is to use mattress stitch to pick up the bars between the columns of stitches.

Working upwards or downwards as preferred, secure yarn to one of the pieces you wish to join. Place the edges of the work together and pick up a bar from one side, then the corresponding bar from the opposite side. Repeat. After a few stitches, pull gently on the yarn and the two sides will come together in a seam that is almost invisible. Take care to stay in the same column all the way. Do not pull the stitches tight at the beginning as you will not be able to see what you are doing.

Garter stitch joins

It is easier to join garter stitch as it has a firm edge and lies flat. Place the edges of the work together, right side up, and see where the stitches line up. Pick up the bottom loops of stitches on one side of the work and the top loops of the stitches on the other side. After a few stitches, pull gently on the yarn. The stitches should lock together and lie completely flat. The inside of the join should look the same as the outside.

Kitchener stitch/ Kitchener grafting

This is a method of grafting stitches invisibly together.

Method

Divide the stitches you wish to join evenly between two double-pointed needles. Hold both needles parallel in your left hand, so that the working yarn is to your right, and is coming off the first stitch on the back needle. Cut the working yarn to a reasonable working length.

- Using a third needle, **purl** the first stitch on the **front** needle.
- Drop the stitch off the left front needle, and pull the yarn all the way through the dropped stitch so that there is no longer a stitch on the right (working) needle.
- **Knit** the next stitch on the **front** needle, but this time leave the stitch on the left front needle and pull the yarn all the way through as before.
- **Knit** the first stitch on the **back** needle.
- Drop the stitch off the left back needle and pull the yarn all the way through.
- **Purl** the next stitch on the **back** needle.
- **Leave** this stitch on the left back needle and pull the yarn all the way through.

Repeat as set until two stitches remain, then work these two stitches together and drop both stitches off the needles. Pull the yarn all the way through and thread on a tapestry needle. Bring yarn to the inside of work and weave in ends, tacking down the last loops as necessary for a neat finish.

Heels & toes

Shaping the toe

There are many different ways of shaping a toe.
This is the most common, and it is guaranteed to work!

Begin with 64 sts divided between three needles (32 sts on N1, 16 sts on N2 and 16 sts on N3).

Round 1: Work to last 3 stitches on N1, k2tog, k1; on N2 k1, skpo, work to last 3 sts, k2tog, k1, on N3 k1, skpo, work to end.

Round 2: K all sts.

Rep last two rounds until 40 sts rem (10/20/10) sts.

Next round: As round 1.

Rep until 20 sts rem (5/10/5) sts) then knit the 5 sts from N1 on to the end of N3 so you have (10 sts on each of two needles).

Using Kitchener Stitch, graft these stitches together.

Wrapping stitches

A wrap stitch is used to eliminate the risk of holes when using the short row shaping method. Work to where the wrap is required, then to work it slip the next stitch on to the right needle, bring the yarn to the front of work between the needles, then slip the same stitch back on to the left needle. On subsequent rows work the loop and the wrapped stitch as k2tog and turn. Continue from pattern.

Easy heel explained

This simple technique for heels works over any even number of stitches. The example below produces a heel suitable for an adult-size sock in standard 4-ply sock yarn.

Example

Cast on 64 stitches on 2.5 mm needles. Work in rounds until the point where the heel is to begin, then divide stitches so that there are 32 on N1, 16 on N2 and 16 on N3. N1 holds the stitches for the top of the foot, while N1 and N3 hold the stitches that will form the heel. To shape the heel, increase 1 st at the beginning of N2 and at the end of N3 on every alternate row. The diagram shows N1 as a green line and N2 and N3 as red lines. The increase points are where N1 meets N2 and N3 or where green meets red.

Note: the number of stitches on N2 and N3 increases from 16 to 30. The number of stitches on N1 remains constant.

Heel decreases

The stitches on N2 and N3 now need to be decreased to shape the heel, leaving 32 stitches on N1. To do this, work across to the last stitch on N1, then on N2 k1, k2tog, k1, turn. (32+1)

Next row Sl1p-wise, p2 on N1, p across the 32 sts on N1, then on N3 p1, p2 tog, p1, turn.

Next row Sl1, k2 on N3, k across 32 sts on N1, then on N2 k1, k2tog, k1, turn.

Cont as set, working back and forth in rows, until there are 16 sts on N2 and 16 sts on N3 (32 sts rem on N1). Cont on these 64 sts down the length of the foot until it measures 3in (7.5cm) less than desired length for socks. Work toe as desired.

- **N1 remains at 32 sts throughout**
- **N3 increases from 16 sts to 30 sts**
- **N2 increases from 16 sts to 30 sts**

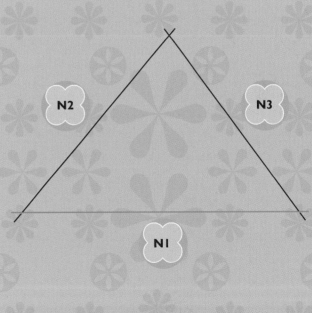

Conversions

Needle sizes

UK	Metric	US
14	2mm	0
13	2.5mm	1
12	2.75mm	2
11	3mm	–
10	3.25mm	3
–	3.5mm	4
9	3.75mm	5
8	4mm	6
7	4.5mm	7
6	5mm	8
5	5.5mm	9
4	6mm	10
3	6.5mm	10.5
2	7mm	10.5
1	7.5mm	11
0	8mm	11
00	9mm	13
000	10mm	15

UK/US Yarn Weights

UK	US
2ply	Lace
3ply	Fingering
4 ply	Sport
Double knitting	Light worsted
Aran	Fisherman/Worsted
Chunky	Bulky
Super chunky	Extra bulky

Abbreviations

approx	approximately
cont	continue
cm	centimetres
d g-st	double garter stitch (2 rounds p, 2 rounds k)
DK	double knitting
foll	following
inc	increase by working twice into stitch
in(s)	inch(es)
k	knit
k-wise	with needles positioned as for working a knit stitch
k2tog	knit two stitches together
M1L	make 1 stitch slanting to the left
M1R	make 1 st slanting to the right
p	purl
p2tog	purl two stitches together
p-wise	with needles positioned as for working a purl stitch
rem	remaining
rep	repeat
RS	right side of work
skpo	slip one, knit one, pass slipped stitch over
ss	slip stitch
ssk	slip one stitch knitwise, then slip 1 st purlwise, then knit the two stitches together through the back of the lookps
ssp	slip one stitch kwise, slip one stitch pwise, then purl sts tog
st(s)	stitch(es)
*	work instructions following * then repeat as directed
( )	repeat instructions inside brackets as directed
WS	wrong side of work
yf	yarn forward
yrn	yarn round needle

I cannot remember a time before knitting,
a time when yarn did not run through my fingers and feature in my life.
I was first recorded knitting at the age of four, along with my darling grandmother
who taught me all she knew about fibres. I knitted through my childhood and teenage
years, gaining a Guides' badge; through long hours of night duty as a student nurse;
in many countries while travelling; through lonely evenings and sad times and through
happy times and my children's childhoods. If stitches were tears I might have knitted
an ocean by now, but just as much of my work has soft memories of golden times
worked into every stitch.

After my introduction to felt-making, I began making things bigger simply to felt them
down to size. Patterns were redefined and yarn trials carried out; I began to push
boundaries by combining materials and techniques in unusual ways. I love
experimenting and adding in other fibres, and choosing colours and yarns is always a
challenge. Knitting is addictive yet calming, helping me to be at one with the ups and
downs of life. Let it into your life and enjoy the journey.

My inspiration comes from nature and my garden in every season, as well as
architecture that arrests my attention as I travel, from a Greek door with peeling paint
to Madrid's prize-winning new airport. All these socks have a story behind them,
and I hope you enjoy making them as much as I enjoyed creating them.

Chrissie Day

Index

GMC Publications would like to thank:

Ann Budd for permission to reproduce her chart on sock
sizing, Gilda Pacitti, Elsa and Ed Clinton, Marc and Mary
Mothersole, Neville Van Sittert and James and Johannes for
their lovely feet.

Shot at The Old Forge, South Heighton, East Sussex, home of
sculptor Christian Funnell (www.christianfunnell.com). It backs on
to the beautiful south downs and is regularly open to the public
as part of art trails (see www.aoh.org.uk) or by prior arrangement.

For knitting tips and enquiries about any of the patterns
in this book visit Chrissie Day's website at:
www.chrissieday.co.uk

Contact us for a complete catalogue, or visit our website:
GMC Publications Ltd, 166 High Street, Lewes, East Sussex BN7 1XU, United Kingdom
Tel: 01273 488005 Fax: 01273 402866
www.gmcbooks.com